easy
Knits for Kids

50 Knit and
Crochet Projects

easy
Knits for Kids

50 Knit and Crochet Projects

Sixth&Spring Books
New York

Sixth&Spring Books
233 Spring Street
New York, NY 10013

Editor-in-Chief
Trisha Malcolm

Book Editor
Michelle Lo

Art Director
Chi Ling Moy

Book Manager
Theresa McKeon

Copy Editor
Daryl Brower

Yarn Editor
Veronica Manno

Technical Editors
Carla Scott
Karen Greenwald

President and Publisher, Sixth&Spring Books
Art Joinnides

Family Circle Magazine
Editor-in-Chief
Susan Kelliher Ungaro

Executive Editor
Barbara Winkler

Creative Director
Diane Lamphron

1 3 5 7 9 8 6 4 2

Library of Congress Catalog-in-Publication Data
Family circle easy knits for kids
        p.cm.
        ISBN 1-931543-15-1 Trade
        ISBN 1-931543-47-X Paper
            1. Knitting--Patterns. 2. Children's clothing. I. Title: Easy knits for kids. II Family
circle (New York, N.Y.)

TT825 .F357 2002
746.43'2043--dc21

                                                                    2002022154

Manufactured in China

Table of Contents

Fall Favorites

These back-to-school classics make great gear for cool kids.

Child's Play
for beginner knitters

Color her world with this striped kid-friendly pullover. Thick and thin bands of hot hues add cheer to a simple A-line style with rolled edges. "Child's Play" first appeared in the Fall '99 issue of *Family Circle Easy Knitting* magazine.

MATERIALS
- *Knitaly*® by Lane Borgosesia, 3¹/₂oz/100g balls, each approx 215yd/194m (wool) 1 ball each in #3799 coral (A), #3821 turquoise (B), #2479 olive (C), #238 yellow (D), #3365 red (E) and #1940 lilac (F)
- One pair size 6 (4mm) needles OR SIZE TO OBTAIN GAUGE
- One each sizes 5 and 6 (3.75 and 4mm) circular needles, 16"/40cm long

SIZES
Sizes for Child's 4 (6, 8, 10, 12). Shown in size 6.

FINISHED MEASUREMENTS
- Chest 30 (32, 35, 37, 40)"/76 (81, 89, 94, 101.5)cm
- Length 15 (17, 18¹/₂, 20¹/₂, 23)"/38 (43, 48, 52, 58)cm
- Upper arm 14 (15¹/₂, 16¹/₂, 18¹/₂, 20¹/₂)"/35.5 (39.5, 42, 47, 52)cm

GAUGE
21 sts and 30 rows to 4"/10cm over St st using size 6 (4mm) needles.
TAKE TIME TO CHECK YOUR GAUGE.

STRIPE PAT
[2 rows each: A, B, C, D, E, F] twice, 14 (16, 18, 20, 22) rows A, 14 (16, 18, 20, 22) rows B, 8 (10, 12, 14, 16) rows C, 2 rows B, 8 (10, 12, 14, 16) rows C, 16 (18, 20, 22, 24) rows D, 8 (10, 12, 14, 16) rows E, 2 rows F, 8 (10, 12, 14, 16) rows E, then cont with F to end of piece.

BACK
With A, cast on 91 (97, 104, 109, 117) sts. Work in St st and stripe pat, dec 1 st each side every 10th (10th, 12th, 14th, 16th) rows 6 times—79 (85, 92, 97, 105) sts. Work even until piece measures 8¹/₂ (10, 11, 12, 13¹/₂)"/22 (25, 28, 30.5, 34)cm, end with a WS row.

Armhole shaping
Bind off 3 sts at beg of next 2 rows, 2 sts at beg of next 2 rows, 1 st at beg of next 4 rows—65 (71, 78, 83, 91) sts. Work even until armhole measures 5³/₄ (6¹/₄, 6³/₄, 7³/₄, 8³/₄)"/14 (16, 18, 19.5, 22)cm, end with a WS row.

Neck shaping
Next row (RS) Work 27 (30, 32, 34, 38) sts, join 2nd ball of yarn and bind off center 11 (11, 14, 15, 15) sts, work to end. Working both sides at once with separate balls of yarn, bind off from each neck edge 5 sts once, 4 sts once. Bind off rem 18 (21, 23, 25, 29) sts each side for shoulders.

FRONT
Work as for back until armhole measures 4¹/₂ (5, 5¹/₂, 6¹/₂, 7¹/₂)"/11 (13, 15, 16.5, 19)cm, end with a WS row.

Neck shaping
Next row (RS) Work 28 (31, 33, 35, 39) sts, join 2nd ball of yarn and bind off center 9 (9, 12, 13, 13) sts, work to end. Working both sides at once with separate balls of yarn, bind off from each neck edge 3 sts once, 2 sts twice, dec 1 st each side every other row 3 times. Work even until same length as back. Bind off rem 18 (21, 23, 25, 29) sts each side for shoulders.

SLEEVES
With A, cast on 52 (52, 55, 55, 58) sts. Work in St st and stripe pat, inc 1 st each side every 4th row 5 (10, 7, 16, 23) times, every 6th row 6 (5, 9, 5, 2) times—74 (82, 87, 97, 108) sts. Work even until piece measures 8¹/₂ (10¹/₄, 12, 13¹/₂, 15)"/22 (26, 30, 34, 38)cm from beg.

Cap shaping
Bind off 3 sts at beg of next 2 rows, 2 sts at beg of next 2 rows, 1 st at beg of next 2 rows, 5 sts at beg of next 6 rows. Bind off rem 32 (40, 45, 55, 66) sts.

FINISHING
Block pieces to measurements. Sew shoulder seams.

Neckband
With RS facing, smaller circular needle and A, pick up and k 81 (81, 87, 90, 90) sts evenly around neck edge. Join and work in k2, p1 rib in foll stripes: 4 rows each A, B, C and D. Change to larger circular needle and cont in St st (k every rnd) as foll: 4 rows E, 4 rows F, 12 rows A. With A, bind off loosely. Set in sleeves. Sew side and sleeve seams.

(See charts on page 127)

Class Act

for intermediate knitters

A cool zip-front cardigan with contrast collar and sleeves earns top grades for form and function. Worked in soft, chunky wool, it looks good and feels great! "Class Act" first appeared in the Fall '97 issue of *Family Circle Easy Knitting* magazine.

MATERIALS

- *Ram's Wool* by Patons/Coats Patons 3½ oz/100g balls, each approx 140yd/128m (wool)
  4 (5, 5, 6) skeins in #3660 black (MC)
  1 (1, 1, 2) skeins in #3638 royal blue (A)
  1 (1, 2, 2) skeins in #3644 dusty blue (B)
- One pair each sizes 8 and 10 (5 and 6mm) needles OR SIZE TO OBTAIN GAUGE
- Stitch markers
- One separating zipper, 14 (15, 16, 17)"/36 (38, 41, 43)cm long

SIZES

Sized for Child's 6 (8, 10, 12). Shown in size 8.

FINISHED MEASUREMENTS

- Chest 34 (36, 38, 40)"/86.5 (91.5, 96.5, 101.5)cm
- Length 18 (18½, 19½, 21)"/46 (47, 49.5, 53.5)cm
- Width at upper arm 15 (16, 17, 18)"/ 38 (41, 43, 46)cm

GAUGES

- 15 sts and 20 rows to 4"/10cm over St st, using larger needles.
- 16 sts and 20 rows to 4"/10cm over chart pat, using larger needles.
TAKE TIME TO CHECK GAUGES.

Note

Use separate bobbins for solid blocks of color in chart. When changing color, bring new yarn under old to twist strands and prevent holes.

BACK

With smaller needles and MC, cast on 66 (70, 74, 78) sts. Work in k2, p2 rib for 1"/2.5cm, end with a WS row. Change to larger needles. Beg and end as indicated for back, work Plaid chart until piece measures 18 (18½, 19½, 21)"/46 (47, 49.5, 53.5)cm from beg. Bind off all sts.

LEFT FRONT

With smaller needles and MC, cast on 33 (33, 37, 37) sts. **Next row (RS)** K2, *p2, k2; rep from * to last 3 sts, end p2, k1. **Next row** K the knit sts and p the purl sts. Rep last row until rib measures 1"/2.5cm, inc 0 (2, 0, 2) sts on last (WS) row—33 (35, 37, 39) sts. Change to larger needles. Beg and end as indicated for left front, work in chart pat until piece measures 15½ (16, 17, 18½)"/ 39.5 (40.5, 43, 47)cm from beg, end with a RS row.

Neck shaping

Next row (WS) Bind off 5 (5, 7, 7) sts (neck edge), work to end. Dec 1 st at neck edge every row 5 times, then every other row twice more—21 (23, 23, 25) sts. Work even until same length as back to shoulder. Bind off.

RIGHT FRONT

Work to correspond to left front, reversing k2, p2 ribbing by working as foll: **Next row (RS)** K1, *p2, k2; rep from * to end. Beg and end chart as indicated for right front.

SLEEVES

With smaller needles and MC, cast on 26 (30, 34, 34) sts. work in k2, p2 rib for 1½"/4cm, inc 4 (4, 2, 4) sts evenly across last (WS) row—30 (34, 36, 38) sts. Change to larger needles. Work in St st with MC, inc 1 st each side every other row 2 (0, 1, 2) times, every 4th row 11 (13, 13, 13) times—56 (60, 64, 68) sts. Work even until piece measures 12½ (13, 13½, 14)"/32 (33, 34, 35.5)cm from beg. Bind off.

FINISHING

Block pieces. Sew shoulder seams.

Right front edging

With RS facing, smaller needles and MC, pick up and k58 (60, 64, 70) sts evenly along right front edge to beg of neck shaping. Bind off all sts knitwise.

Left front edging

Work to correspond to right front edging.

Collar

With RS facing, smaller needles and MC, beg at right front neck edge and pick up and k16 (16, 18, 18) sts evenly along right front neck, 24 (24, 28, 28) sts along back neck, inc 2 sts evenly across, 16 (16, 18, 18) sts evenly along left front neck edge—58 (58, 66, 66) sts. Beg with a WS row and p2, work in k2, p2 rib for 4½"/11.5cm. Bind off loosely in rib. Fold collar in half to WS and sew in place. Sew collar edges tog.

Pocket lining and edging

Place markers on side edges of front and back, with the first marker 1"/2.5cm above top of ribbing, and the 2nd marker 4"/10cm above first marker. With RS facing, larger needles and MC, pick up and k16 sts between markers on

(Continued on page 126)

Girl Talk

for beginner knitters

This great-looking pair—an easy fitting turtleneck and always-right short-sleeved pullover—gets A's in style. Make a quick work of both in simple stockinette stitch and ribbed edging. "Girl Talk" first appeared in the Fall '00 issue of *Family Circle Easy Knitting* magazine.

MATERIALS

Turtleneck Pullover
- *Tweedy* by Filatura Di Crosa/ Tahki·Stacy Charles, 1³/₄oz/50g balls, each approx 154yd/140m (wool)
  5 (6, 7) balls in #78 cream
- One pair each sizes 4 and 6 (3.5 and 4mm) needles OR SIZE TO OBTAIN GAUGE
- Sizes 4 and 6 (3.5 and 4mm) circular needles, 16"/40cm long

Short-sleeved Pullover
- *Butterfly* by Filatura Di Crosa/ Tahki·Stacy Charles, 1³/₄oz/50g balls, each approx 192yd/175m (mohair/acrylic)
  4 (5, 6) balls in #411 khaki
- One pair each sizes 6 and 8 (4 and 5mm) needles OR SIZE TO OBTAIN GAUGE
- Size 6 (4mm) circular needle, 16"/40cm long

Short sleeve Pullover
- *Cotton Classic* by Tahki·Stacy Charles, 1³/₄oz/50g balls, each approx 108yd/100m (cotton)
  2 (2, 3) balls each in #3003 natural (A) and #3211 khaki (B)
- One pair each sizes 4 and 6 (3.5 and 4mm) needles OR SIZE TO OBTAIN GAUGE
- Size 4 (3.5mm) circular needle, 16"/40cm long
- Cable needle

TURTLENECK PULLOVER

SIZES
Sized for Child's 6 (8, 10). Shown in size 8

FINISHED MEASUREMENTS
- Chest 30 (33, 36)"/76 (84, 91.5)cm
- Length 16¹/₂ (18, 19¹/₄)"/42 (45.5, 49)cm
- Upperarm 11¹/₄ (13, 14¹/₂)"/28.5 (33, 37)cm

GAUGE
17 sts and 28 rows to 4"/10cm over St st using larger needles.
TAKE TIME TO CHECK YOUR GAUGE.

BACK
With smaller needles, cast on 64 (70, 76) sts. Work in k2, p2 rib for 2¹/₂"/6.5cm. Change to larger needles and work in St st until piece measures 8¹/₂ (9¹/₂, 10¹/₄)"/21.5 (24, 26)cm from beg.

Armhole shaping
Bind off 2 sts at beg of next 4 rows, dec 1 st each side every other row 2 (2, 3) times—52 (58, 62) sts. Work even until armhole measures 7 (71/2, 8)"/18 (19, 20.5)cm.

Shoulder and neck shaping
Bind off 4 (5, 5) sts at beg of next 4 rows, 5 (5, 6) sts at beg of next 2 rows, AT SAME TIME, bind off center 12 (14, 16) sts for neck and working both sides at once, bind off 4 sts from each neck edge once, 3 sts once.

FRONT
Work as for back until armhole measures 5¹/₂ (6, 6¹/₂)"/14 (15, 16.5)cm, end with a WS row.

Neck and shoulder shaping
Next row (RS) Work 21 (23, 24) sts, join 2nd ball of yarn and bind off center 10 (12, 14) sts, work to end. Working both sides at once, bind off from each neck edge 3 sts once, 2 sts once, dec 1 st every other row 3 times, AT SAME TIME, when same length as back to shoulder, shape shoulder as for back.

SLEEVES
With smaller needles, cast on 36 (40, 44) sts. Work in k2, p2 rib for 2¹/₂"/6.5cm. Change to larger needles and work in St st, inc 1 st each side every 10th row 6 (8, 9) times—48 (56, 62) sts. Work even until piece measures 13 (15, 16¹/₂)"/33 (38, 42)cm from beg.

Cap shaping
Bind off 3 sts at beg of next 2 rows, 2 sts at beg of next 4 rows, dec 1 st each side every other row 8 times, every 4th row twice, bind off 3 sts at beg of next 2 rows, 2 sts at beg of next 2 rows. Bind off rem 4 (12, 18) sts.

FINISHING
Block pieces to measurements. Sew shoulder seams.

(Continued on page 127)

Great Investment

for advanced knitters

Practice your stitching skills on a two-tone Aran vest. This V-neck classic, worked in a textural medley of lattice, honeycomb and twisted cables, will give your needles a workout without making too many demands of your time. "Great Investment" first appeared in the Fall '00 issue of *Family Circle Easy Knitting* magazine.

MATERIALS

- *Cotton Classic* by Tahki•Stacy Charles, 1¾oz/50g balls, each approx 108yds/100m (cotton)
  2 (2, 3) balls each in #3003 natural (A) and #3211 khaki (B)
- One pair each sizes 4 and 6 (3.5 and 4mm) needles OR SIZE TO OBTAIN GAUGE
- Size 4 (3.5mm) circular needle, 16"/40cm long
- Cable needle

SIZES

Sized for Child's 6 (8/10,12). Shown in size 8/10.

FINISHED MEASUREMENTS

- Chest 35 (39, 41)"/89 (99, 104)cm
- Length 17¾ (19½, 21½)"/45 (50, 54.5)cm

GAUGES

- 24 sts and 34 rows to 4"/10cm over rice st using larger needles.
- 31 sts and 34 rows to 4"/10cm over cable pats using larger needles.

TAKE TIME TO CHECK YOUR GAUGES.

RICE STITCH

Row 1 (RS) P1, *k1, p1; rep from * to end.
Row 2 Knit.
Rep rows 1 and 2 for rice st.

STRIPE PATTERN

6 rows A, 4 rows B, 6 rows A, 4 rows B.
stitches used

2-st RT

Skip next st and k 2nd st in front of first st, then k first st, drop both sts from LH needle.

4-st RC

Sl 2 sts to cn and hold to back, k2, k2 from cn.

4-st LC

Sl 2 sts to cn and hold to front, k2, k2 from cn.

4-st RPC

Sl 2 sts to cn and hold to back, k2, p2 from cn.

4-st LPC

Sl 2 sts to cn and hold to front, p2, k2 from cn.

8-st RC

Sl 4 sts to cn and hold to back, k4, k4 from cn.

8-st LC

Sl 4 sts to cn and hold to front, k4, k4 from cn.

BACK

With smaller needles and B, cast on 134 (146, 158) sts. Work in k1, p1 rib for 1¼"/3cm. Change to larger needles.

Beg pats

Row 1 (RS) Work 11 (17, 23) sts rice st, 4 sts rev St st, 15 sts chart 1, 2 sts rev St st, 8 sts chart 2, 3 sts rice st, 8 sts chart 3, 2 sts rev St st, 28 sts chart 4, 2 sts rev St st, 8 sts chart 2, 3 sts rice st, 8 sts chart 3, 2 sts rev St st, 15 sts chart 1, 4 sts rev St st, 11 (17, 23) sts rice st. Cont in pats as established until piece measures 6½ (7½, 8¼)"/17 (19, 21)cm from beg. Work 20 rows stripe pat, then cont with A to end of piece, AT SAME TIME, when piece measures 10 (11, 12)"/25.5 (28, 30.5)cm from beg, work as foll:

Armhole shaping

Bind off 3 sts at beg of next 2 rows, 2 sts at beg of next 2 rows, dec 1 st each side every other row twice—120 (132, 144) sts. Work even until armhole measures 7 (7¾, 8¾)"/17.5 (20, 22)cm.

Shoulder and neck shaping

Bind off 12 (14, 16) sts at beg of next 2 rows, 11 (12, 13) sts at beg of next 4 rows, AT SAME TIME, bind off center 32 (36, 40) sts for neck and working both sides at once, bind off 5 sts from each neck edge twice.

FRONT

Work as for back until armhole measures 2¾ (3, 3½)"/7 (8, 9)cm, end with a WS row.

Neck shaping

Next row (RS) Work 60 (66, 72) sts, join 2nd ball of yarn and work to end. Work 1 row even.
Next row Work to last 4 sts of first half, k3tog, k1; on 2nd half, k1, SK2P, work to end. Work 1 row even. Rep last 2 rows 5 times more.
Next row Work to last 3 sts of first half, k2tog, k1; on 2nd half, k1, SKP, work to end. Work 1 row even. Rep last 2 rows 13 (15, 17) times more, AT SAME TIME, when same length as back to shoulder, shape shoulder as for back.

FINISHING

Block pieces to measurements. Sew shoulder and side seams.

Neckband

With RS facing, circular needle and A, pick up and k 142 (150, 158) sts evenly around neck edge. Join and mark 1 st in center of V-neck. Work in rnds of k1, p1 rib as foll: Next rnd Rib to 1 st before center st at V-neck, sl 2 knitwise (as for a k2tog), k1, pass 2 sl sts over k st (for 2-st

(Continued on page 128)

Blue Mood

for beginner knitters

A cozy cardigan is sure to lift spirits on a less-than-perfect day. Veronica Manno's relaxed design features a purl ridge at underarms and single-crochet edging. A simple pin closure makes a fine finish. "Blue Mood" first appeared in the Fall '01 issue of *Family Circle Easy Knitting* magazine.

MATERIALS

- *Baby* by Tahki Yarns/Tahki•Stacy Charles, Inc. 3½oz/100g balls each approx 60yd/55m (wool)
  3 (4, 4, 5) balls in #5 lt blue
- One pair size 13 (9mm) needles OR SIZE TO OBTAIN GAUGE
- Size J/10 (6.5mm) crochet hook
- One large decorative safety pin
- Stitch holders

SIZES

Sized for Child's 4 (6, 8, 10). Shown in size 4.

FINISHED MEASUREMENTS

- Chest 28 (30½, 32, 34½)"/71 (77.5, 81, 87.5)cm
- Length 11½ (12½, 14, 15½)"/29 (32, 35.5, 39.5)cm
- Upper arm 11 (12, 13, 14)"/28 (30.5, 33, 35.5)cm

GAUGE

10 sts and 14 rows to 4"/10cm over St st using size 13 (9mm) needles.
TAKE TIME TO CHECK YOUR GAUGE.

BACK

Cast on 35 (38, 40, 43) sts. K 2 rows. Then cont in St st until piece measures 5½ (6, 7, 8)"/14 (15, 18, 20.5)cm from beg, end with a WS row. P 1 row on RS (for ridge at yoke). Work even until piece measures 11½ (12½, 14, 15½)"/29 (32, 35.5, 39.5)cm from beg.

Shoulder and neck shaping

Bind off 12 (13, 14, 15) sts at beg of next 2 rows. Sl center 11 (12, 12, 13) sts to a holder for back neck.

LEFT FRONT

Cast on 18 (20, 21, 23) sts. K 2 rows. Then cont in St st until piece measures same length as back to ridge at yoke. P 1 row on RS for ridge. Work even until same length as back to shoulder.

Shoulder shaping

Next row (RS) Bind off 12 (13, 14, 15) sts, sl rem 6 (7, 7, 8) sts to a holder for front neck.

RIGHT FRONT

Work to correspond to left front, reversing shaping. Sew shoulder seams.

SLEEVES

Beg and end just above yoke ridge, from RS pick up and k 30 (32, 35, 37) sts along armhole edge. Work in St st dec, 1 st each side every 6th row 3 (4, 5, 5) times, every 4th row 3 (2, 2, 3) times—18 (20, 21, 21) sts. Work even until sleeve measures 9½ (10½, 11½, 12½)"/24 (26.5, 29, 32)cm. P 1 row on RS. Bind off knitwise.

FINISHING

Block to measurements.

COLLAR

Work across sts from holders and pick up and k 3 sts at each shoulder seam—29 (32, 32, 35) sts. Work in St st, inc 1 st each side every other row twice—33 (36, 36, 39) sts. Work even until collar measures 4"/10cm. Bind off. Sew side and sleeve seams. With crochet hook, work an edge of sc evenly along center fronts and all around collar edge. Use safety pin to close front at yoke edge.

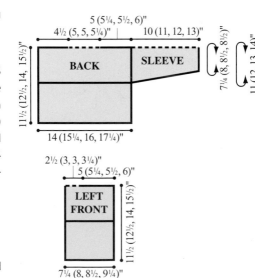

Game Day
for beginner knitters

Score lots of points with Abigail Liles's rough-and-tumble pullover. Worked in simple stockinette with garter ridges, this striped sensation will stand up to all your little soccer star can dish out. "Game Day" first appeared in the Fall '97 issue of *Family Circle Knitting* magazine.

MATERIALS
- *Lambs Pride Superwash Bulky* by Brown Sheep 3½ oz/100g, each approx 110yd/100m (wool)
  2 balls in #SW82 red sable (A)
  2 (2, 3, 3) balls each in #SW52 emerald city (B), #SW92 blue heaven (C), #SW27 mysterious fuchsia (D), #SW93 ocean sky (E)
- One pair size 10 (6mm) needles OR SIZE TO OBTAIN GAUGE
- Size 9 (5½mm) circular needle 16"/40cm long
- Stitch holders and markers

SIZES
Sized for Child's 4 (6, 8,10). Shown in size 6.

FINISHED MEASUREMENTS
- Chest 34 (36, 37, 38)"/86.5 (91.5, 94, 96.5)cm
- Length 19½ (20, 20½, 21)"/49.5 (51, 52, 53.5)cm
- Width at upper arm 15 (16, 17, 18)"/38 (40.5, 43, 46)cm

GAUGE
16 sts and 21 rows to 4"/10cm using larger needles in Stripe pat.
TAKE TIME TO CHECK GAUGE

STRIPE PAT
*K 2 rows A, 10 rows St st with B, k 2 rows A, 10 rows St st with C, k2 rows A, 10 rows St st with D, k 2 rows A, 10 rows St st with E; rep from * (48 rows) for Stripe pat.

BACK
With larger needles and A, cast on 68 (72, 74, 76) sts. Work in Stripe pat until piece measures 19½ (20, 20½, 21)"/49.5 (51, 52, 53.5)cm from beg, end with a WS row. **Next row (RS)** Bind off 21 (22, 23, 24) sts, place center 26 (28, 28, 28) sts on holder, join 2nd ball of yarn bind off rem sts.

FRONT
Work as for back until piece measures 17½ (18, 18½, 19)"/44.5 (46, 47, 48)cm from beg, end with a WS row.

Neck shaping
Next row (RS) K 28 (29, 30, 31) sts, place center 12 (14, 14, 14) sts on a holder, join 2nd ball of yarn, work to end. Working both sides at once, bind off from each neck edge 2 sts 3 times, dec 1 st at each neck edge every other row once. When same length as back, bind off rem 21 (22, 23, 24) sts each side.

SLEEVES
With larger needles and A, cast on 32 (36, 36, 36) sts. Work in Stripe pat, inc 1 st each side every other row 0 (0, 4, 8) times, every 4th row 14 (14, 12, 10) times—60 (64, 68, 72) sts. Work even until piece measures 12"/30.5cm from beg. Bind off.

FINISHING
Block pieces. Sew shoulder seams.

Neckband
With circular needle and A, beg at left shoulder and pick up and k 10 sts along left front neck edge, 12 (14, 14, 14) sts from front neck holder, 10 sts along right front neck edge, 26 (28, 28, 28) sts from back neck holder — 58 (62, 62, 62) sts. Join, place marker, p 1 rnd. Change to C and k 8 rnds. Change to A and k 1 rnd. Bind off all sts purlwise. Place marker 7½ (8, 8½, 9)"/19 (20.5, 21.5, 23)cm down from shoulders on front and back. Sew sleeves between markers. Sew side and sleeve seams.

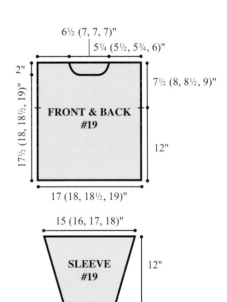

FRONT & BACK #19

6½ (7, 7, 7)"
5¼ (5½, 5¾, 6)"
2"
17½ (18, 18½, 19)"
7½ (8, 8½, 9)"
12"
17 (18, 18½, 19)"

SLEEVE #19

15 (16, 17, 18)"
12"
8 (9, 9, 9)"

Red Hot
for beginner knitters

A high-voltage hue turns Teva Durham's basic turtleneck into something flashy and fresh. This timeless silhouette combines standard and reverse stockinette stitching with a textural thick-and-thin yarn. "Red Hot" first appeared in the Fall '01 issue of *Family Circle Easy Knitting* magazine.

MATERIALS
- *Woolspun* by Lion Brand Yarn Co, 1¾oz/50g balls, each approx 100yd/91m (cotton) 4 (4, 5, 6) balls in #142 wine
- Size 13 (9mm) circular needle, 24"/60cm long OR SIZE TO OBTAIN GAUGE
- Size 10 (6mm) circular needle, 16"/40cm long
- Stitch markers
- Stitch holder

SIZES
Sized for Child's 8 (10, 12, 14). Shown in size 10.

FINISHED MEASUREMENTS
- Chest 28½ (30, 32, 34)"/72.5 (76, 81, 86)cm
- Length 16½ (18, 19, 19½)"/42 (45.5, 48, 49.5)cm
- Upper arm 12 (13¼, 14½, 15½)"/30.5 (33.5, 37, 39.5)cm

GAUGE
10 sts and 14 rnds (or rows) to 4"/10cm over St st using larger circular needle.
TAKE TIME TO CHECK YOUR GAUGE.

Note
Body of pullover is worked in one piece on circular needle to armhole.

BODY
With larger circular needle, cast on 72 (76, 80, 86) sts. Join, pm to mark beg of rnd.
Rnd 1 P20 (21, 22, 24), k32 (34, 36, 38), p20 (21, 22, 24). Work even in St st and reverse St st blocks as established until piece measures 11 (12, 12½, 12½)"/28 (30.5, 32, 32)cm from beg.
Divide for armholes
Next rnd P20 (21, 22, 24), k 16 (17, 18, 19) and sl these sts to a holder for front to be worked later.

BACK
Cont across rem sts, k1 (selvage st), k2tog, k13

(14, 15, 16), p17 (18, 19, 21), p2tog, k1 (selvage st), turn. Work 1 row even as established.
Next row (RS) K1, k2tog, work to last 3 sts, p2tog, k1. Rep last 2 rows twice more—28 (30, 32, 35) sts. Work even until armhole measures 5½ (6, 6½, 7)"/14 (15, 16.5, 18)cm. Bind off.

FRONT
Return to sts on holder and work armhole dec's as on back—28 (30, 32, 35) sts. Work even until armhole measures 3½ (4, 4½, 5)"/9 (10, 11.5, 12.5)cm.
Neck shaping
Next row (RS) Work 10 (11, 11, 12) sts, join a 2nd ball of yarn and sl center 8 (8, 10, 11) sts to a holder for neck, work to end. Working both sides at once, dec 1 st each side of neck edge every other row 3 times—7 (8, 8, 9) sts rem each side. Work even until same length as back. Bind off sts each side for shoulders.

RIGHT SLEEVE
With larger circular needle, cast on 22 (23, 24, 25) sts. Working back and forth in rows, work in St st inc 1 st each side every 10th (10th, 8th, 8th) row 4 (5, 6, 7) times—30 (33, 36, 39) sts. Work even until piece measures 13½ (15, 16 ½ 17½)"/34 (38, 42, 44.5)cm from beg.
Cap shaping
Dec 1 st each side of next RS row then every other row 3 times more—22 (25, 28, 31) sts. Bind off.

LEFT SLEEVE
Working in reverse St st, work as for right sleeve.

FINISHING
Block pieces to measurements. Sew shoulder seams.
Collar
With smaller circular needle, pick up and k 36 (36, 40, 42) sts evenly around neck edge. Join and work in rnds of k1, p1 rib for 4½"/11.5cm. Bind off in rib with larger needle. Sew sleeves into armholes. Sew side and sleeve seams.

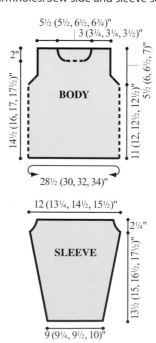

Boy Band
for beginner knitters

Deep ribs and muted colors blend in perfect harmony on this zippy pullover. Worked in sporty stripes, this quick-stitch knit will take center stage wherever your little star may go. "Boy Band" first appeared in the Fall '00 issue of *Family Circle Easy Knitting* magazine.

MATERIALS
- *Knitaly®* by Lane Borgosesia, 3½ oz/100g balls, each approx 215yd/195m (wool)
  2 (2, 3) balls in #20426 grey (MC)
  1 ball each in #41249 lt green (A) and #41257 brick (B)
- One pair each sizes 5 and 7 (3.5 and 4.5mm) needles OR SIZE TO OBTAIN GAUGE
- 5"/12cm zipper

SIZES
Sized for Child's 2 (4/6, 8). Shown in size 4/6.
FINISHED MEASUREMENTS
- Chest 29 (32½, 37)"/73.5 (83.5, 94)cm
- Length 13 (14½, 16)"/33 (37, 40.5)cm
- Upper arm 11 (12, 13)"/28 (31, 33)cm

GAUGE
26 sts and 28 rows to 4"/10cm over rib pat (slightly stretched) using larger needles.
TAKE TIME TO CHECK YOUR GAUGE.

STITCHES USED
k2, p1 rib
(multiple of 3 sts plus 2)
Row 1 (RS) *K2, p1; rep from *, end k2.
Row 2 K the knit sts and p the purl sts.
Rep rows 1 and 2 for k2, p1 rib.
rib pattern
(multiple of 6 sts plus 5)
Row 1 (RS) *K5, p1; rep from *, end k5.
Row 2 K1, p3, k1, *k2, p3, k1; rep from * to end.
Rep rows 1 and 2 for rib pat.

STRIPE PATTERN
2 rows B, 2 rows MC, 4 rows A, 2 rows MC, 10 rows A, 2 rows MC, 4 rows A, 2 rows MC, 2 rows B.

BACK
With smaller needles and A, cast on 95 (107, 119) sts. Work in k2, p1 rib for 3 rows. Change to MC and cont rib until piece measures 1½"/4cm from beg, end with a WS row. Change to larger needles and work in rib pat until piece measures 5½ (6½, 7)"/14 (16.5, 18)cm from beg. Cont in rib pat and work 30 rows stripe pat. Cont with MC only until piece measures 13 (14½, 16)"/33 (37, 40.5)cm from beg. Bind off all sts.

FRONT
Work as for back until piece measures 9 (10½, 12)"/23 (27, 30.5)cm from beg, end with a WS row.
Placket shaping
Next row (RS) Work 47 (53, 59) sts, join 2nd ball of yarn and bind off center st, work to end. Work both sides at once until placket measures 2"/5cm.
Neck shaping
Bind off from each neck edge 6 (7, 8) sts once, 3 sts once, 2 sts once, 1 st 3 times. Work even until same length as back. Bind off rem 33 (38, 43) sts each side for shoulders.

SLEEVES
With smaller needles and A, cast on 47 (53, 53) sts. Work in k2, p1 rib as for back. Change to larger needles and work in rib pat, inc 1 st each side (working inc sts into rib pat) every other row 9 (5, 6) times, every 4th row 3 (8, 10) times—71 (79, 85) sts, AT THE SAME TIME, when piece measures 2½ (4, 5½)"/6.5 (10, 14)cm from beg, work 30 rows of stripe pat, then 2 rows MC—piece should measure 7 (8½, 10)"/17.5 (21.5, 25.5)cm from beg. Bind off all sts.

FINISHING
Block pieces to measurements. Sew shoulder seams.
Collar
With RS facing, smaller needles and MC, pick up and k 83 (89, 92) sts evenly around neck edge. Work in k2, p1 rib for 2½"/6cm. Change to A and rib 2 rows. Bind off in rib with A.
Place markers 5½ (6, 6½)"/14 (15.5, 16.5)cm down from shoulders on front and back for armholes. Sew top of sleeves between markers. Sew side and sleeve seams. Sew in zipper.

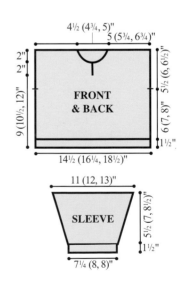

Weekend Wonder

for intermediate knitters

Jump on the fast track to great style with Mari Lynn Patrick's fast-knitting mock-turtleneck. This sassy sleeveless top gets its incredible texture from thick-and-thin yarn and simple stitches. "Weekend Wonder" first appeared in Fall '00 issue of *Family Circle Easy Knitting* magazine.

MATERIALS
■ *Fiamma* by DiVé/Lane Borgosesia, 1³/₄oz/50g balls, each approx 55yd/50m (wool)
   7 (7, 8, 9) balls in #17146 lavender multi
■ One pair size 11 (8mm) needles OR SIZE TO OBTAIN GAUGE
■ Stitch markers

SIZES
Sized for X-Small (Small, Medium, Large).
Shown in size Small.

FINISHED MEASUREMENTS
■ Lower edge 33 (35, 37, 39)"/84 (89, 94, 99)cm
■ Waist 28 (30, 32, 34)"/71 (76, 81, 86)cm
■ Bust 32 (34, 36, 38)"/81 (86, 91.5, 96.5)cm
■ Length 20 (20¹/₂, 21, 21¹/₂)"/51 (52, 53, 54.5)cm

GAUGE
12 sts and 17 rows to 4"/10cm over St st using size 11 (8mm) needles.
TAKE TIME TO CHECK YOUR GAUGE.

BACK
Cast on 50 (53, 56, 59) sts. Work in k1, p1 rib for 4 rows. Cont in St st until piece measures 3"/7.5cm from beg. **Dec row (RS)** K11 (12, 13, 14), pm, SKP, k to last 13 (14, 15, 16) sts, k2tog, pm, k11 (12, 13, 14). Rep dec row, dec 1 st after first marker and before second marker every 4th row 3 times more—42 (45, 48, 51) sts. Work even for 5 rows. **Inc row (RS)** Inc 1 st after first marker and before second marker. Rep inc row every 6th row twice more—48 (51, 54, 57) sts. Work even until piece measures 11¹/₂"/29cm

from beg. **Next row (RS)** [K1, p1] 4 times, k to last 8 sts, [p1, k1] 4 times. Cont to work as established with 8 sts each side in rib for 3 rows more.

Armhole shaping
Bind off 3 sts at beg of next 2 rows. **Dec row (RS)** [P1, k1] twice, p1, SKP, k to last 7 sts, k2tog, [p1, k1] twice, p1. Rep dec row every other row twice more—36 (39, 42, 45) sts. Work even until armhole measures 6¹/₂ (7, 7¹/₂, 8)"/16.5 (18, 19, 20.5)cm.

Shoulder shaping
Bind off 5 sts at beg of next 2 (4, 2, 0) rows, 4 (0, 6, 6) sts at beg of next 2 (0, 2, 4) rows. Bind off rem 18 (19, 20, 21) sts for back neck.

FRONT
Work as for back until armhole measures 5 (5¹/₂, 6, 6¹/₂)"/12.5 (14, 15, 16.5)cm.

Neck shaping
Next row (RS) Work 14 (15, 16, 17) sts, join 2nd ball of yarn and bind off center 8 (9, 10, 11) sts, work to end. Working both sides at once, bind off 2 sts from each neck edge once, dec 1 st every other row 3 times—9 (10, 11, 12) sts rem each side. When same length as back, shape shoulders as for back.

FINISHING
Block pieces to measurements. Sew one shoulder seam.

Turtleneck
Pick up and k 49 (51, 53, 55) sts evenly around neck edge. Work in k1, p1 rib for 2¹/₂"/6.5cm. Bind off in rib. Sew other shoulder and turtleneck seam. Sew side seams.

6 (6¹/₄, 6¹/₂, 7)"
2¹/₄ (2¹/₂, 2³/₄, 3)"
2¹/₂"
1"
6¹/₂ (7, 7¹/₂, 8)"
17¹/₂ (18, 18¹/₂, 19)"
FRONT & BACK
5¹/₄"
4¹/₄"
3"
16¹/₂ (17 ¹/₂, 18¹/₂, 19¹/₂)"
14 (15, 16, 17)"
16 (17, 18, 19)"

Zip it Up!

for intermediate knitters

Mari Lynn Patrick's hooded zip-front jacket packs a punch. Perked up with three bands of pretty patterning, it will be at the top of her "must-have" list. "Zip it Up!" first appeared in the Fall '01 issue of *Family Circle Easy Knitting* magazine.

MATERIALS
- *Red Heart® Soft* by Coats & Clark, 5oz/140g skeins, each approx 328yd/302m (acrylic)
  - 3 (4, 4) skeins in #7744 dk red (A)
  - 1 (1, 1) skeins in #7012 black (B)
- One pair each sizes 6 and 8 (4 and 5mm) needles OR SIZE TO OBTAIN GAUGE
- 18"/45cm separating zipper
- Stitch holders

SIZES
Sized for Child's 10 (12, 14). Shown in size 12.

FINISHED MEASUREMENTS
- Chest 34 (36, 38)"/86 (91.5, 96.5)cm
- Length 21 (21½, 22)"/53 (54.5, 56)cm
- Upper arm 12 (13, 13½)"/30.5 (33, 34)cm

GAUGE
19 sts and 26 rows to 4"/10cm over St st using larger needles.
TAKE TIME TO CHECK YOUR GAUGE.

BACK
With smaller needles and A, cast on 81 (85, 91) sts. Work in k1, p1 rib for 2½"/6.5cm, inc 1 st each side of last WS row—83 (87, 93) sts.

Beg chart 1
Row 1 (RS) K1 (selvage st), beg with st 10 (8, 5), work to end of chart, then work 11-st rep, end with st 2 (4, 7), k1 (selvage st). Cont to foll chart through row 10. Then with A, work in St st for 14 rows more.

Beg chart 2
Row 1 (RS) K1, beg with st 3 (1, 10), work to end of chart, then work12-st rep, end with st 11 (1, 4), k1. Cont to foll chart through row 19. With A, work 1 row even. Piece measures 11"/28cm from beg.

Raglan armhole shaping
Note
With A, cont in St st for 2½"/6.5cm or 16 rows.

Then, work 10 rows of chart 1 and cont with A to end of piece. Bind off 2 sts at beg of next 2 rows.
Dec row (RS) K1, SKP, k to last 3 sts, k2tog, k1. Rep dec row every other row 22 (24, 26) times more—33 (33, 35) sts.
Next row (RS) K1, SK2P, k to last 4 sts, k3tog, k1. Work 1 row even. Rep last 2 rows once more—25 (25, 27) sts. Sl these sts to a holder.

RIGHT FRONT
Note
Make right front first to center pats at center front. With smaller needles and A, cast on 41 (43, 47) sts. Work in k1, p1 rib for 2½"/6.5cm, inc 1 st each side of last WS row— 43 (45, 49) sts.

Beg chart 1
Row 1 (RS) K1 (selvage st), beg with st 1, work 11-st rep across, end with st 8 (10, 3), k1 (selvage st). Cont to foll chart through row 10. Then with A, work in St st for 14 rows more.

Beg chart 2
Row 1 (RS) K1, beg with st 1, work 12-st rep across, end with st 5 (7, 11), k1. Cont to foll chart through row 19. With A, work 2 rows even.

Armhole shaping
Note
Work armhole with A as on back and beg chart row 1 on same row as back, beg with st 1 of chart.
Next row (WS) Bind off 2 sts, work to end. **Dec row 1 (RS)** K to last 3 sts, k2tog, k1. Rep dec row

1 every other row 17 (19, 21) times more.
Dec row 2 (RS) K to last 4 sts, k3tog, k1. Rep dec row 2 every other row 3 times more, AT SAME TIME, when there are 25 (25, 27) sts and center front edge measures 18"/45.5cm, beg neck shaping.

Neck shaping
Next row (RS) Bind off 5 sts, work to end. Cont to shape neck binding off 3 sts from neck edge every other row 0 (0, 2) times, 2 sts 5 (5, 3) times.

LEFT FRONT
Work to correspond to right front, centering all pats at center front (foll right front) and reversing all shaping.

RIGHT SLEEVE
With smaller needles and A, cast on 37 (37, 39) sts. Work in k1, p1 rib for 2½"/6.5cm, inc 1 st each side of last WS row—39 (39, 41) sts. Change to larger needles and inc 1 st each side every 6th row 10 (12, 13) times, AT SAME TIME, when 4 (5, 6)"/10 (12.5, 15)cm are worked in St st OR 26 (32, 38) rows, work 10 rows chart 1 pat, centering pat, then work 2½"/6.5cm with A, then 2 rows foll chart 2, centering pat. Work 1 row even with A. Piece measures approx 14 (15, 16)"/35.5 (38, 40.5)cm from beg. There are 59 (63, 67) sts.

(Continued on page 128)

Farm Fresh

for intermediate knitters

Old McDonald had a farm, and on his farm he had some… well, a little of everything! Perky piglets and dapper ducks make cute companions on this playful pullover; additional details include contrast-colored edging and bright stripes. Designed by Susan Guagliumi, "Farm Fresh" first appeared in the Fall '99 issue of *Family Circle Easy Knitting* magazine.

MATERIALS
- *Anti-Tickle DK* by King Cole/Classic Elite Yarns, 1¾oz/50g balls, each approx 123yd/112m (wool)
  - 3 (4, 4) skeins #26 blue (MC)
  - 1 (2, 2) skeins #142 brown (A)
  - 1 skein each #94 pink (B), #23 dk brown (C), #165 pale green (D), #39 tan (E) and #55 yellow (F)
  - Small amount #48 black (G)
- One pair each sizes 3 and 5 (3 and 3.75mm) needles OR SIZE TO OBTAIN GAUGE
- Size 3 (3mm) circular needle, 16"/40cm long
- Size E/4 (3.5mm) crochet hook
- 3 small black buttons or beads for eyes
- Bobbins

SIZES
Sized for Girl's 2 (4, 6). Shown in size 4.

FINISHED MEASUREMENTS
- Chest 26 (28, 30)"/66 (71, 76)cm
- Length 13½ (15, 16½)"/34 (38, 42)cm
- Upper arm 13 (14, 15)"/33 (35, 38)cm

GAUGE
22 sts and 30 rows to 4"/10cm over St st using larger needles.
TAKE TIME TO CHECK YOUR GAUGE.

Notes
1 Use a separate bobbin of yarn for each block of color. When changing colors, twist yarns on WS to prevent holes in work.
2 If desired, small areas of color can be worked in duplicate st after pieces are knit.
3 Sun rays are worked in stem stitch.

BACK
With smaller needles and MC, cast on 73 (77, 83) sts and work in garter st as foll: 3 rows MC, 4 rows D, 4 rows E and 4 rows A. Change to larger needles. Beg with a p row, work in St st for 3 (5, 11) rows with A. Beg and end as indi-cated, work rows 1-74 of back chart, then cont with MC only until piece measures 13½ (15, 16½)"/34 (38, 42)cm from beg. Bind off all sts.

FRONT
Work as for back, working 1 (3, 9) rows in St st with A above garter st before working chart, and work front chart through row 66 (72, 76). Piece measures approx 10½ (11½, 13)"/26.5 (29, 33)cm from beg.

Neck shaping
Next row (RS) Work 34 (35, 38) sts, join 2nd ball of yarn and bind off center 5 (7, 7) sts, work to end. Working both sides at once with separate balls of yarn, bind off from each neck edge 3 sts 3 times, 2 sts once, dec 1 st every other row once, every 4th row twice. Work even until same length as back. Bind off rem 20 (21, 24) sts each side for shoulders.

SLEEVES
With smaller needles and MC, cast on 41 (45, 49) sts and work garter st as for back. Change to larger needles and beg with a p row, work in St st and stripes as foll: 13 rows A, 2 rows C, 5 rows E, [2 rows C, 5 rows D] twice, 2 rows C, 5 rows MC, 2 rows C, then cont with MC to end of sleeve, AT SAME TIME, inc 1 st each side every 4th row 14 (13, 12) times, every 6th row 2 (3, 5) times—73 (77, 83) sts Work even until piece measures 11½ (12, 13)"/29 (30.5, 33)cm from beg. Bind off all sts.

FINISHING
Block pieces to measurements. Sew shoulder seams.

Neckband
With RS facing, circular needle and MC, pick up and k 78 (84, 84) sts evenly around neck edge. Join and work in garter st (k 1 rnd, p 1 rnd) in foll stripes: 3 rnds MC, 4 rnds D, 4 rnds E, 3 rnds A. Bind off knitwise with A.
Place markers 6½ (7, 7½)"/16.5 (17.5, 19)cm down from shoulder seams on front and back for armholes. Sew top of sleeves between markers. Sew side and sleeve seams. Embroider sun rays with F using stem st.

Large ear
With RS facing, larger needle and B, pick up 10 sts (see chart for placement). Work in St st for 4 rows. Dec 1 st each side on next row, then every other row until there are 2 sts. Bind off.

(Continued on page 129)

Winter Warmers

From traditional to contemporary, sassy sweaters fire up the season.

Bouclé Pullover

for beginner knitters

Kangaroo pockets and a roomy fit are sure to make Victoria Mayo's hooded pullover one of his winter-weather favorites. Textural yarn and rawhide lacing add an edge of casual cool. "Bouclé Pullover" first appeared in the Fall '97 issue of *Family Circle Knitting* magazine.

MATERIALS

- *Landscape* by Naturally 1³/₄oz/50g skeins, each approx 90yd/83m (wool/poly) 10 (12, 14, 15) skeins in #805
- One pair size 13 (9mm) needles OR SIZE TO OBTAIN GAUGE
- Size H/7 (5mm) crochet hook
- Stitch markers
- 24"/61cm leather cord for tie

SIZES

Sized for Child's 4 (6, 8, 10). Shown in size 4.

FINISHED MEASUREMENTS

- Chest 32 (33¹/₂, 37, 38¹/₂)"/81 (85, 94, 98)cm
- Length 17 (18¹/₂, 20, 21¹/₂)"/43 (47, 51, 54.5)cm
- Width at upper arm 13 (14, 16, 17)"/33 (35.5, 40.5, 43)cm

GAUGE

10 sts and 14 rows to 4"/10cm over rev St st, using size 13 (9mm) needles and 2 strands of yarn held tog.
TAKE TIME TO CHECK GAUGE.

Note Pullover is worked with 2 strands of yarn held tog throughout.

BACK

Cast on 40 (42, 46, 48) sts. Work in rev St st (p on RS rows, k on WS rows) until piece measures 17 (18¹/₂, 20, 21¹/₂)"/43 (47, 51, 54.5)cm from beg. Bind off all sts.

FRONT

Work as for back until piece measures 12 (13¹/₂, 14¹/₂, 15¹/₂)"/30.5 (34, 37, 39.5)cm from beg, end with a WS row.

Placket shaping

Next row (RS) Work 20 (21, 23, 24) sts, join 2nd skein and work to end. Cont to work both sides at once until placket measures 3 (3, 3¹/₂, 4)"/7.5 (7.5, 9, 10)cm, end with a WS row.

Neck shaping

Next row (RS) *Work to end of first half; on 2nd half, bind off 4 (4, 5, 5) sts, work to end.*
Next row (WS) Rep from * to *. Cont to bind off from each neck edge 2 sts twice. Work even until same length as back to shoulders. Bind off rem 12 (13, 14, 15) sts each side.

SLEEVES

Cast on 20 (21, 22, 24) sts. Work in rev St st, inc 1 st each side every 4th row 0 (2, 6, 4) times, every 6th row 6 (5, 3, 5) times—32 (35, 40, 42) sts. Work even until piece measures 12 (12, 13, 14)"/30.5 (30.5, 33, 35.5)cm from beg. Bind off all sts.

POCKET

Cast on 28 sts. Work in rev St st for 3¹/₂"/9cm, end with a WS row. Dec 1 st each side every row 3 times, then every other row 5 times. Bind off rem 12 sts.

FINISHING

Block pieces. Sew shoulder seams.

Hood

With RS facing, pick up and k8 (8, 9, 9) sts evenly along right front neck edge, 8 (8, 9, 9) sts along back neck to center back, place marker, pick up and k8 (8, 9, 9) sts along rem half of back neck, 8 (8, 9, 9) sts along left front neck—32 (32, 36, 36) sts. Work in rev St st for 3 rows, sl marker every row. **Next row (RS)** Work to marker, M1 (insert LH needle from front to back under strand bet st just worked and next st on LH needle; k this strand through back loop), sl marker, M1, work to end—34 (34, 38, 38) sts. Cont in pat, working M1 at each side of center marker every 4th row 2 (4, 1, 3) times, then every 6th row 1 (0, 2, 1) times—40 (42, 44, 46) sts. Work even until piece measures 10 (10¹/₂, 11, 11)"/25.5 (26.5, 28, 28)cm. Bind off all sts. Sew pocket onto front, beg 1"/2.5cm from lower edge and centered side to side. Place marker 6¹/₂ (7, 8, 8¹/₂)"/16.5 (18, 20.5, 21.5)cm down from shoulders on front and back for armholes. Sew sleeves between markers. Sew side seams. Sew sleeve seams, reversing seam at lower edge for roll-back cuff. Sew hood seam. With crochet hook and single strand of yarn, work single crochet around edge of hood and along lower edges of body and sleeves.

(See schematics on page 130)

Afterschool Specials

for beginner knitters

Give them a break in classic comfort. His crewneck complements her standout turtleneck. Both knits get a tweedy look from two stands of chunky yarn held together as you knit. The "Afterschool Specials" first appeared in the Fall '01 issue of *Family Circle Easy Knitting* magazine.

MATERIALS

Boy's sweater
- *8 Ply* by Wool Pak Yarns NZ/Baabajoes Wool Co, 8oz/250g balls, each approx 525yd/484m (wool)
  2 (2, 2, 3) balls in black (A) and 2 (2, 2, 3) balls in blue (B)

Girl's sweater
- 2 (2, 2, 2) balls in black (A) and 2 (2, 2, 2) balls in natural (B)
- One pair each sizes 9 and 10½ (5.5 and 6.5mm) needles OR SIZE TO OBTAIN GAUGE
- Stitch holders
- Safety pins

SIZES

For both versions
Sized for Child's 8 (10, 12, 14). Shown in size 12.

FINISHED MEASUREMENTS

Boy's version
- Chest 34 (36, 38½, 40½)"/86 (91.5, 98. 103)cm
- Length 19 (20½, 21½, 22)"/48 (52, 54.5, 56)cm
- Upper arm 15 (16, 17, 18)"/38 (41, 43, 46)cm

Girl's version
- Chest 36 (37½, 40, 42½)"/91.5 (95, 101.5, 108)cm
- Length 20½ (21½, 23, 23¾)"/52 (54.5, 58.5, 60)cm
- Upper arm 14½ (14½, 15½, 17)"/37 (37, 39.5, 43)cm

GAUGE

For both versions
13 sts and 18 rows to 4"/10cm over St st using 1 strand each A and B held tog and larger needles.
TAKE TIME TO CHECK YOUR GAUGE.

Note

Work with 1 strand each A and B held tog throughout for both sweater.

BOY'S SWEATER

BACK

With smaller needles and 1 strand A and B, cast on 57 (59, 63, 67) sts. Work in k1, p1 rib for 1½"/4cm, dec 1 (0, 0, 1) st on last WS row—56 (59, 63, 66) sts. Change to larger needles and cont in St st until piece measures 19 (20½, 21½, 22)"/48 (52, 54.5, 56)cm from beg. Bind off.

FRONT

Work as for back until piece measures 16½ (18, 19, 19½)"/42 (45.5, 48, 49.5)cm from beg.

Neck shaping

Next row (RS) K24 (25, 27, 28), join another 2 balls of yarn and bind off center 8 (9, 9, 10) sts, k to end. Working both sides at once, bind off 2 sts from each neck edge 3 times—18 (19, 21, 22) sts rem each side. Work even until same length as back. Bind off.

SLEEVES

With smaller needles and 1 strand A and B, cast on 27 (27, 29, 29) sts. Work in k1, p1 rib for 2"/5cm, dec 0 (1, 0, 1) st on last row—27 (26, 29, 28) sts. Change to larger needles and cont in St st inc 1 st each side every 4th row 11 (13, 13, 15) times—49 (52, 55, 58) sts. Work even until piece measures 13 (14, 15, 16)"/33 (35.5, 38, 40.5)cm from beg. Bind off.

FINISHING

Block pieces to measurements. Sew one shoulder seam.

Neckband

With smaller needles and 1 strand A and B, pick up and k 65 (67, 67, 69) sts evenly around neck edge. Work in k1, p1 rib for 3"/7.5cm. Bind off knitwise. Sew other shoulder seam. Fold neckband in half to RS and sew in place. Place markers at 7½ (8, 8½, 9)"/19 (20.5, 21.5, 23)cm down from shoulders. Sew sleeves to armholes between markers. Sew side and sleeve seams.

GIRL'S SWEATER

BACK

With smaller needles and 1 strand A and B, cast on 59 (61, 65, 69) sts. Work in k1, p1 rib for 2"/5cm. Change to larger needles and cont in St st until piece measures 11 (12, 12½, 12½)"/28 (30.5, 32, 32)cm from beg.

Raglan armhole shaping

Bind off 2 sts at beg of next 2 rows.

Dec row (RS) K3, k3tog, k to last 6 sts, SK2P, k3. Rep dec row every 4th row 8 (8, 9, 10) times more—19 (21, 21, 21) sts. Sl these sts to a holder.

FRONT

Work as for back until a total of 7 (7, 8, 9) dec rows have been worked in raglan armhole and there are 27 (29, 29, 29) sts. Work 1 row even.

Neck shaping

Next row (RS) Work 10 sts, join a 2nd ball of yarn and k7 (9, 9, 9) sts and place these sts on a holder, k to end. Working both sides at once, rep dec row on next RS row then every 4th row once more—4 sts rem each side. Sl these 4 sts

(Continued on page 131)

Bear Necessity

for intermediate knitters

Linda Cyr's shoulder-buttoned jumper is designed to delight. Knit in soft pink in an easy twisted rib pattern, it's accented with a cuddly intarsia panda-bear motif. "Bear Necessity" first appeared in the Winter '96/'97 issue of *Family Circle Knitting* magazine.

MATERIALS

- *Cotton Fleece* by Brown Sheep 3½oz/100g each skein approx 215yd/197m
  2 (2, 3, 3) skeins of #230 pink (MC)
  1 skein each #160 brown (A) and #150 cream
- One pair size 6 (4mm) needles OR SIZE TO OBTAIN GAUGE
- Two 1"/25cm buttons
- Tapestry needle

SIZES

Sized for 4 (6, 8, 10). Shown in size 6.

FINISHED MEASUREMENTS

- Chest 23 (25, 27½, 30)"/58.5 (63.5, 70, 76)cm
- Length (not including straps) 18 (21, 22¾, 23¼)"/46 (53.5, 58, 59)cm

GAUGE

20 sts and 28 rows to 4"/10cm over St st using size 6 (4mm) needles.
TAKE TIME TO CHECK YOUR GAUGE.

BACK

With MC, cast on 75 (83, 91, 99) sts. Work k1, p1 rib for 4 rows. **Next row (RS)** Knit. **Next row** P 5, [k1, p7] 8 (9, 10, 11) times, k1, p5. Rep last 2 rows until piece measures 4¼ (5, 5½, 5¾)"/11 (12.5, 14, 14.5)cm above ribbing, end with a WS row. **Dec row** K3, [ssk, k6] 8 (9, 10, 11) times, ssk, k6—66 (73, 80, 87) sts. **Next row** P5 [k1, p6] 8 (9, 10, 11) times, k1, p4. **Next row** Knit. Rep last 2 rows until piece measures 4¼ (5, 5½, 5¾)"/11 (12.5, 14, 14.5)cm above last dec row, end with a WS row. **Dec row** K5, [k2tog, k5] 8 (9, 10, 11) times, k2tog, k3—57 (63, 69, 75) sts. **Next row** P4, [k1, p5] 8 (9, 10, 11) times, k1, p4. **Next row** Knit. Rep last 2 rows until piece measures 13½ (16, 17½, 18)"/34 (40.5, 44.5, 46)cm from beg, end with a WS row.

Armhole shaping

Bind off 4 (5, 6, 7) sts at beg of next 2 rows. Dec 1 st each side every row 5 times, every other row once, every 4th row once—35 (39, 43, 47) sts. Work even until armhole measures 4 (4½, 4¾, 4¾)"/10 (11.5, 12, 12)cm, end with a WS row. Work in k1, p1 rib for 4 rows. Bind off.

FRONT

Work as for Back until piece measures 8¾ (10¾, 12¾, 13¾)"/22 (27.5, 32.5, 35)cm from beg, end with a WS row. Place markers each side of center 41sts. Work Teddy Bear motif in St st foll chart and work rem sts in pat st with MC, through chart row 49, AT SAME TIME, when piece measures same length as back to underarm, work armhole shaping as for back. Work until armhole measures 4 (4½, 4¾, 4¾)"/10 (11.5, 12, 12)cm, ending with a WS row. Work in k1, p1 rib for 4 rows. Work a 4-st buttonhole (bind off 4 sts; then cast on 4 sts over these bound-off sts on next row) 2 sts in from the armhole edge on each side on the first row. Bind off.

STRAPS (make 2)

With MC, cast on 8 sts. **Row 1** Knit. **Row 2** K1, p6, k1. Rep rows 1 & 2 until strap measures desired length. Bind off.

FINISHING

Block pieces. Sew side seams. Sew straps to back at base of top ribbing. Try jumper on child for button placement or sew buttons approx 1½"/4cm from strap edge. Embroider face on teddy bear as pictured.

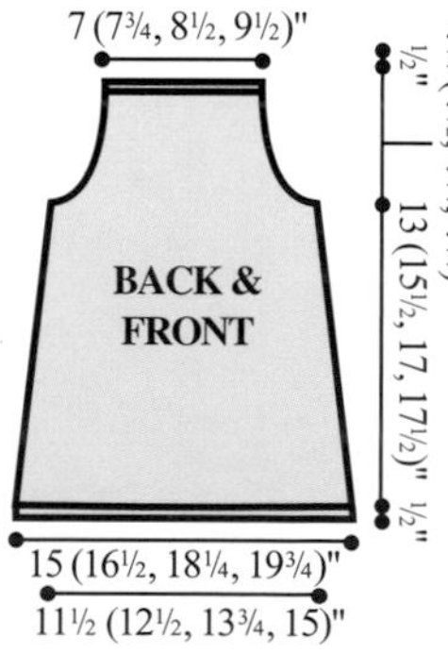

7 (7¾, 8½, 9½)"
4¼ (4½, 4¾, 4¾)"
½"
13 (15½, 17, 17½)"
½"
BACK & FRONT
15 (16½, 18¼, 19¾)"
11½ (12½, 13¾, 15)"

(See chart on page 131)

Fair Play

for intermediate knitters

Let the good times roll with a color-charged sweater and scarf set. Agi Revesz updates a traditional Fair Isle design in an all-over stitch pattern accented with snowflake motifs and a bright band inspired by traditional Nordic knits. "Fair Play" first appeared in the Winter '97/'98 issue of *Family Circle Knitting* magazine.

MATERIALS

- *Red Heart Classic* by Coats & Clark 3½oz/100g skeins, each approx 198yd/183m (acrylic)
  4 (4, 5) skeins in #401 grey (MC),
  1 skein each in #1 white (A), #12 black (B) and #912 red (for girl's) or #848 blue (for boy's) (C)
- One pair each sizes 7 and 8 (4.5 and 5mm) needles OR SIZE TO OBTAIN GAUGE

SIZES

Sized for 4 (6, 8). Both shown in size 6.

FINISHED MEASUREMENTS

- Chest 30 (31½, 35)"/76 (80, 89)cm
- Length 16½ (17½, 19½)"/42 (44.5, 49.5)cm
- Width at upper arm 13 (14, 15)"/33 (35.5, 38)cm

Scarf
- Width 8"/20.5cm
- Length 52"/32cm

GAUGE

17 sts and 26 rows to 4"/10cm over Pat st, using larger needles.
TAKE TIME TO CHECK GAUGE.

STITCHES USED

Pat st (multiple of 4 sts, plus 3)
Row 1 (RS) *K3, p1; rep from *, end k3.
Rows 2 and 4 Purl.
Row 3 K1, *p1, k3; rep from *, end p1, k1.
Rep rows 1-4 for Pat st.

BACK

With smaller needles and MC, cast on 63 (67, 75) sts. K 8 rows. Change to larger needles. K 1 row on RS. P 1 row. Work in Pat st until piece measures 6½ (7, 8½)"/16.5 (18, 21.5)cm from beg, end with a WS row. Beg Chart A **Row 1 (RS)** Beg as indicated, work 8-st rep of Chart A across row, end as indicated. Cont in chart pat as estab-lished, AT SAME TIME, when piece measures 10 (10½, 12)"/25.5 (26.5, 30.5)cm from beg, end with a WS row.

Armhole shaping

Cont in chart pat, bind off 3 sts at beg of next 2 rows. Dec 1 st each side on next row, then every other row once more—53 (57, 65) sts. Work even through chart row 42, then cont to rep rows 37-42 of chart until armhole measures 6½ (7, 7½)"/16.5 (18, 19)cm from beg. Bind off all sts.

FRONT

Work as for back until piece measures 15 (16, 17½)"/38 (40.5, 44.5)cm from beg, end with a WS row.

Neck shaping

Next row (RS) Work in pat across 22 (24, 26) sts, join 2nd skein of yarn and bind off center 9 (9, 13) sts, work in pat to end. Working both sides at once, bind off from each neck edge 4 sts once, 3 sts once, then dec 1 st at each neck edge every other row twice. Work even until same length as back. Bind off rem 13 (15, 17) sts each side.

SLEEVES

With smaller needles and MC, cast on 31 (31, 35) sts. K 8 rows. Change to larger needles. K 1 row on RS. P 1 row. Work in Pat st, AT SAME TIME, inc 1 st each side (working inc sts into pat) every 6th row 12 (14, 15) times—55 (59, 65) sts. Work even until piece measures 13 (14, 15)"/33 (35.5, 38)cm from beg, end with a WS row.

Cap shaping

Bind off 5 sts at beg of next 2 rows, 3 sts at beg of next 6 rows. Bind off rem 27 (31, 37) sts.

FINISHING

Block pieces. Sew right shoulder seam.

Neckband

With RS facing, smaller needles and MC, beg at left front shoulder and pick up and k62 (62, 74) sts evenly around neck edge. K 6 rows. Bind off loosely. Sew left shoulder seam, including neck-band. Set in sleeves. Sew side and sleeve seams.

SCARF

Note Work 3 sts each side in garter st for entire length of scarf, working 2 extra rows of garter st band each side every 8th row as foll: ***Next row** [K3, turn] twice, k3 work in pat to end; rep from * once more. With smaller needles and MC, cast on 33 sts. K 8 rows. Change to larger needles. Keeping 3 sts each side in garter st (see note above), work rem 27 sts as foll: K 1 row. P 1 row. Work 4 rows in Pat st. Beg and ending as indicated for scarf, work rows 1-36 of Chart A, then work in Pat st until piece measures 43½"/110.5cm from beg, end with a WS row.

(See charts and schematics on page 130)

Snow White

for intermediate knitters

Special occasions call for a special sweater. Designed by Mari Lynn Patrick, this sweet sleeveless turtleneck is trimmed with a sparkly sequined heart. "Snow White" first appeared in the Winter '99/'00 issue of *Family Circle Easy Knitting* magazine.

MATERIALS

▢ *Chateau* by Reynolds/JCA, 1³/₄oz/50g balls, each approx 136yd/125m (wool/nylon/angora)
  5 (5, 6, 7) balls in #01 white
▢ One pair each sizes 7 and 9 (4.5 and 5.5mm) needles OR SIZE TO OBTAIN GAUGE
▢ One set (4) size 7 (4.5mm) dpn
▢ 1 bag transparent seed beads
▢ Approx 150 iridescent ¹/₂"/15mm sequins
▢ Stitch holders
▢ Five ¹/₂"/15mm buttons

SIZES
Sized for Child's 2 (4, 6, 8). Shown in size 4.

FINISHED MEASUREMENTS
▢ Chest 25 (27, 29, 31)"/63.5 (68.5, 73.5, 78.5)cm
▢ Length 13 (14, 15, 17)"/33 (35.5, 38, 43)cm

GAUGE
15 sts and 23 rows to 4"/10cm over St st using larger needles.
TAKE TIME TO CHECK YOUR GAUGE.

BACK
With smaller needles, cast on 41 (45, 49, 53) sts. Work in k1, p1 rib for 3"/7.5cm, inc 6 sts evenly on last WS row—47 (51, 55, 59) sts. Change to larger needles and cont in St st until piece measures 8 (8¹/₂, 9, 10¹/₂)"/20.5 (21.5, 23, 26.5)cm from beg.

Armhole shaping
Bind off 4 sts at beg of next 2 rows, 2 sts at beg of next 2 rows, dec 1 st each side of next row then every other row 3 (3, 3, 4) times more—27 (31, 35, 37) sts. Work even until armhole measures 4¹/₂ (5, 5¹/₂, 6)"/11.5 (12.5, 14, 15)cm.

Neck shaping
Next row (RS) K8 (10, 12, 12), join 2nd ball of yarn and bind off center 11 (11, 11, 13) sts, work to end. Working both sides at once, bind off 2 sts from each neck edge once. When armhole measures 5 (5¹/₂, 6, 6¹/₂)"/12.5 (14, 15,

16.5)cm, bind off rem 6 (8, 10, 10) sts each side for shoulders.

FRONT
Work as for back until armhole measures 2¹/₂ (3, 3¹/₂, 4)"/6.5 (7.5, 9, 10)cm.

Neck shaping
Next row (RS) K11 (13, 15, 15), join 2nd ball of yarn and bind off center 5 (5, 5, 7) sts, work to end. Working both sides at once, bind off 2 sts from each neck edge once, 1 st every other row 3 times. When same length as back, bind off rem 6 (8, 10, 10) sts each side for shoulders.

FINISHING
Block pieces to measurements. Sew shoulder seams.

Armhole bands
With RS facing and smaller needles, pick up and k 50 (54, 60, 64) sts evenly around each armhole. Work in k1, p1 rib for 1¹/₂"/4cm. Bind off in rib.

Neckband
With RS facing and dpn, pick up and k 58 (58, 58, 62) sts evenly around neck edge. Join and work in rnds of k1, p1 rib for 5¹/₂"/14cm. Bind off in rib.

Heart Embroidery
Using heart template, enlarge 200% and transfer outline to front of top with basting stitches.

Using one seed bead at the center of one sequin, sew on beaded sequins to front of top inside a heart (see diagram). Sew side seams.

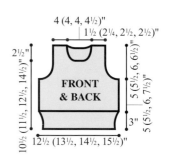

Multiple Choice

for intermediate knitters

Look on the bright side with crayon-colored sweaters and a fanciful matching hat. Her zip-front pullover, designed by Mary Lou Eastman, sports spirited stripes; his version, designed by Astor Mui, favors bold color blocks. The matching multi-colored hat, designed by Lila Chin, can be topped with I-cord or a playful pompom. "Multiple Choice" first appeared in the Winter '97/'98 issue of *Family Circle Easy Knitting* magazine.

MATERIALS

Boy's sweater

- *Canadiana* by Patons 3½oz/100g skeins, each approx 228 yd/208m (acrylic) 1 skein each in #3 black (A), #141 light blue (B), #58 willow (C), #81 gold (D) and #143 med. blue (E)

Girl's sweater

  1 skein each in #3 black (A), #5 cardinal (B), #143 med. blue (C), #81 gold (D), #3503 green (E) and #119 teal (F)

Both sweaters

- One pair size 7 (4.5mm) needles OR SIZE TO OBTAIN GAUGE
- Stitch holders and markers
- 6"/15cm black zipper

Hat

- 1 skein each in #3 black (A), #141 lt blue (B), #58 willow (C), #81 gold (D) and #143 med. Blue (E)
- Five size 7 (4.5mm) double-pointed needles (dpn) OR SIZE TO OBTAIN GAUGE
- Stitch markers

SIZES

Both sweaters sized for Child's 2 (4, 6). Shown in size 6. Hat is sized fit 2-6.

FINISHED MEASUREMENTS

Both sweaters

- Chest 28 (30, 32)"/71 (76, 81) cm
- Length 14 (16, 18)"/35.5 (40.5, 46)cm
- Width at upper arm 13 (14, 15)"/33 (35.5, 38)cm

Hat

- Circumference 22-24"/51-53cm

GAUGE

Both sweaters

18 sts and 26 rows to 4"/10cm over St st, using size 7 (4.5mm) needles.

Hat

18 sts and 26 rows to 4"/10cm over St st, using size 7 (4.5mm) needles.

TAKE TIME TO CHECK GAUGE.

BOY'S SWEATER

STITCHES USED

Stripe pat

Work in St st in foll color sequence: *10 rows B, 10 rows C, 2 rows A, 10 rows D, 10 rows E, 2 rows A; rep from * (44 rows) for Stripe pat.

BACK

With A, cast on 64 (68, 72) sts. Beg with a WS row, k 7 rows. Then work in Stripe pat until piece measures 13 (15, 17)"/33 (38, 43)cm from beg, end with a WS row.

Shoulder shaping

Bind off 7 sts at beg of next 4 rows, 7 (7, 8) sts at beg of next 2 rows. Bind off rem 22 (26, 28) sts.

FRONT

Work as for back until piece measures 5 (7, 8¾)"/12.5 (18, 22)cm from beg, end with a WS row.

Placket shaping

Next row (RS) K 29 (31, 33), join A and k 6 sts, join 2nd skein of stripe color, k to end. Cont in Stripe pat, working center 6 sts in garter st with A, for 5 rows more. Divide for zipper opening:
Next row (RS) K to center 6 sts, k 3 with A, join 2nd skein of A and k 3, k to end in established Stripe pat. Working both sides at once, work even until piece measures 11¾ (13¾, 15½)"/30 (35, 39.5)cm from beg, end with a WS row.

Neck shaping

Next row (RS) Work all sts of left front in pat; on right front, k 3 with A and place these sts on a holder to be worked later, bind off next 4 sts, k in pat to end. **Next row** P to end of right front; on left front, place first 3 sts on a holder, bind off next 4 sts, p to end. Cont working both sides at once, dec 1 st at each neck edge every row 1 (3, 3) times, then every other row 3 (3, 4) times, AT SAME TIME, when same length as back to shoulders, shape shoulders each side as for back.

(Continued on page 132)

Penguin Parade

for intermediate knitters

Intarsia penguins lend a touch of winter whimsy to cozy zippered coverups. A white panel showcases the little waddlers front and back on her version; on his, they dance playfully around the cuffs. "Penguin Parade" first appeared in the Winter '98/'99 issue of *Family Circle Easy Knitting* magazine.

MATERIALS

- *Anti-Tickle DK* by King Cole/Cascade Yarns, 1¾oz/50g balls each approx 123yd/112m (wool)

Boy's sweater

- 4 (5, 6, 7) balls in #21 royal (A)
- 2 balls in #1 white (B) and 1 ball each in #48 black (C), #9 red (D) and #63 teal (E)
- Small amount in #55 yellow (F)
- One 9 (10, 12, 14)"/22 (25, 30, 35)cm blue separating zipper

Girl's sweater

- 4 (5, 6, 7) balls in #21 royal (A), 2 balls in #1 white (B) and 1 ball each in #48 black (C),
- Small amounts each in #9 red (D), #63 teal (E) and #55 yellow (F)
- One 10 (12, 14, 16)"/25 (30, 35, 40)cm blue separating zipper

Both sweaters

- One pair each sizes 7 and 9 (4.5 and 5.5mm) needles OR SIZE TO OBTAIN GAUGE
- Size G/6 (4.5mm) crochet hook
- Bobbins
- Stitch markers

SIZES

Boy's sweater

Sized for Child's 2 (4, 6, 8). Shown in size 6.

Girl's sweater

Sized for Girl's sizes 2 (4, 6, 8). Shown in size 4.

FINISHED MEASUREMENTS

Boy's sweater

- Chest 29 (31, 33, 35)"/73.5 (78.5, 84, 89)cm
- Length 13½ (15, 17, 19)"/34.5 (38.5, 43, 48)cm
- Upper arm 11 (12, 13, 14)"/28 (31, 33, 35)cm

Girl's sweater

- Chest (closed) 27¼ (29¼, 31¼, 33¼)"/69 (74.5, 79.5, 84.5)cm
- Length 13½ (15, 17, 19)"/34.5 (38.5, 43, 48)cm
- Upper arm 11 (12, 13, 14)"/28 (31, 33, 35)cm

GAUGE

Both sweaters

16 sts and 24 rows to 4"/10cm over St st and 2 strands of yarn held tog using larger needles. TAKE TIME TO CHECK YOUR GAUGE.

BOY'S SWEATER

Notes

1 Work with 2 strands of a color held tog throughout.

2 When working charts, read RS rows from right to left and WS rows from left to right, unless otherwise indicated.

3 When changing colors, twist yarns on WS to prevent holes.

BACK

With smaller needles and 2 strands A, cast on 58 (62, 66, 70) sts. Work in k1, p1 rib for 1½"/4cm. Change to larger needles. Beg with a k row, work in St st for 4 rows.

Beg boy's chart 1

Next row (RS) Work first st of chart, work 4-st rep 14 (15, 16, 17) times, work last st of chart. Cont as established until 13 rows of chart have been worked, then cont in St st with A only until piece measures 8 (9, 10½, 12)"/20.5 (23, 26.5, 30.5)cm from beg.

Armhole shaping

Bind off 3 (3, 4, 4) sts at beg of next 2 rows. Dec 1 st each side on next row, then every other row 1 (2, 2, 3) times more—48 (50, 52, 54) sts. Work even until armhole measures 1 (1½, 2, 2½)"/2.5 (4, 5, 6)cm, end with a WS row.

Beg boy's chart 1

Next row (RS) Work first 0 (1, 0, 1) st of chart, work 4-st rep 12 (12, 13, 13) times, work last 0 (1, 0, 1) st of chart. Cont as established until 13 rows of chart have been worked once, then rep rows 3-13 once, then cont with A only until armhole measures 5½ (6, 6½, 7)"/14 (15.5, 16.5, 17.5)cm. Bind off.

LEFT FRONT

With smaller needles and 2 strands A, cast on 28 (30, 32, 34) sts. Work in k1, p1 rib for 1½"/4cm. Change to larger needles.

Beg boy's chart 1

Next row (RS) Work first 0 (1, 0, 1) st of chart,

work 4-st rep 7 (7, 8, 8) times, work last 0 (1, 0, 1) st of chart. Cont as established until 13 rows of chart have been worked once, then cont with A only until same length as back to armhole. Shape armhole at side edge only (beg of RS rows) as for back—23 (24, 25, 26) sts. Work even until armhole measures 1 (1, 1½, 2)"/2.5 (2.5, 4, 5)cm, end with a WS row.

Neck shaping

Next row (RS) Work to last 2 sts, k2tog (neck dec). Cont to dec 1 st at neck edge every other row 7 (8, 8, 9) times more, AT SAME TIME, when armhole measures 1 (1½, 2, 2½)"/2.5 (4, 5, 6)cm, work 24 rows of chart 1 same as for back, then work with A until same length as back. Bind off rem 15 (15, 16, 16) sts for shoulder.

RIGHT FRONT

Work to correspond to left front, reversing all shaping.

LEFT SLEEVE

With smaller needles and 2 strands A, cast on 30 (32, 34, 36) sts. Work in k1, p1 rib for 1½ (1½, 2, 2)"/4 (4, 5, 5)cm, inc 3 (1, 3, 1) sts on last WS row—33 (33, 37, 37) sts. Change to larger needles. Beg with a k row, work in St st for 4 rows.

Beg boy's chart 2

Next row (RS) Work first 2 (2, 0, 0) sts of chart, work first 4-st rep 2 (2, 3, 3) times, work center 13 sts once, work last 4-st rep 2 (2, 3, 3) times, work last 2 (2, 0, 0) sts of chart. Cont as established until 40 rows of chart have been worked, then cont with A to end of piece, AT SAME TIME, inc 1 st each side (working inc sts into 4-st rep each side) every 6th row 0 (4, 0, 5) times, then every 8th row 6 (4, 8, 5) times—45 (49, 53, 57) sts. Work even until piece measures 11 (12, 14, 15)"/28 (30.5, 35.5, 38)cm from beg.

Cap shaping

Work armhole shaping as for back. Bind off rem 35 (37, 39, 41) sts.

RIGHT SLEEVE

Work as for left sleeve, but reverse direction of penguin on chart 2, by reading the RS rows from left to right and WS rows from right to left.

FINISHING

Block pieces to measurements. Sew shoulder seams. With RS facing, crochet hook and 2 strands A, work 1 row sc evenly around right front, back neck and left front edge. Do not turn. Work 1 row backwards sc (from left to right) in each sc. Sew zipper to fronts. Set in sleeves. Sew side and sleeve seams. With single strand F, embroider bullion st for feet and beak foll chart for placement. With crochet hook and single strand F, ch 20. Tie in a bow and sew to penguin's neck.

GIRL'S SWEATER

Notes

1 Work with 2 strands of a color held tog throughout.

2 When working charts, read RS rows from right to left and WS rows from left to right, unless otherwise indicated.

3 When changing colors, twist yarns on WS to prevent holes.

BACK

With smaller needles and 2 strands A, cast on 53 (57, 61, 65) sts. Work in k1, p1 rib for 1½"/4cm. Change to larger needles.

Beg girl's chart 1

Next row (RS) Work first 2 (0, 2, 0) sts of chart, work first 4-st rep 2 (3, 3, 4) times, work center 33 sts, work last 4-st rep 2 (3, 3, 4) times, work last 2 (0, 2, 0) sts of chart. Cont as established through row 34.

Beg girl's chart 2

Next row (RS) Work 5 (7, 5, 7) sts A, work 8-st rep of chart 5 (5, 6, 6) times, work last 3 sts of chart, work 5 (7, 5, 7) sts A. Cont as established through row 24, then work rows 1-8 once more, then cont with A only to end of piece, AT SAME TIME, when piece measures 8 (9, 10½, 12)"/20.5 (23, 26.5, 30.5) cm from beg, work as foll:

Armhole shaping

Bind off 3 (4, 4, 4) sts at beg of next 2 rows. Dec 1 st each side on next row, then every other row 2 (2, 3, 3) times more—41 (43, 45, 49) sts.

Work even until armhole measures 5½ (6, 6½, 7)"/14 (15.5, 16.5, 17.5)cm. Bind off all sts.

LEFT FRONT

With smaller needles and 2 strands A, cast on 27 (29, 31, 33) sts. Work in k1, p1 rib for 1½"/4cm. Change to larger needles.

Beg girl's chart 1

Next row (RS) Work first 2 (0, 0, 2) sts of chart, work first 4-st rep 1 (2, 2, 2) times, work center 13 sts, work last 4-st rep twice, work last 0 (0, 2, 2) sts of chart. Cont as established through row 34.

Beg girl's chart 2

Next row (RS) Work 3 (5, 7, 1) sts A, work 8-st rep of chart 3 (3, 3, 4) times. Cont as established through row 24, then work rows 1-8 once more, then cont with A only to end of piece, AT SAME TIME, when same length as back to armhole, shape armhole at side edge only (beg of RS rows) as for back—21 (22, 23, 25) sts. Work even until armhole measures 2 (3, 3½, 4)"/5 (7.5, 9, 10)cm, end with a WS row.

Neck shaping

Next row (RS) Work to last 2 sts, k2tog (neck dec). Cont to dec 1 st at neck edge every row 0 (4, 4, 7) times, then every other row 9 (6, 6, 4) times. When same length as back, bind off rem 11 (11, 12, 13) sts for shoulder.

RIGHT FRONT

Cast on and work to correspond to left front, reversing chart placement (reverse direction of penguin on chart 1 by reading the RS rows from left to right and the WS rows from right to left). Reverse all shaping.

SLEEVES

With smaller needles and 2 strands A, cast on 29 (31, 33, 35) sts. With D, k 1 row on RS, then work 1 row in k1, p1 rib. Rep last 2 rows, but in foll color stripes: 2 rows E, 4 rows A, 2 rows E, 2 rows D. Change to larger needles.

Beg girl's chart 2

Next row (RS) Work 1 (2, 3, 0) sts A, work 8-st rep of chart 3 (3, 3, 4) times, work last 3 sts of chart, work 1 (2, 3, 0) sts A. Cont as established, inc 1 st each side (working inc sts into chart pat) every 6th row 8 (9, 10, 11) times—45 (49, 53, 57) sts.

Work even until piece measures 11¼ (13, 14¾, 14¾)"/28.5 (33, 37.5, 37.5)cm from beg.

Cap shaping

Work armhole shaping as for back. Bind off rem 33 (35, 37, 41) sts.

FINISHING

Block pieces to measurements. Sew shoulder seams. With RS facing, crochet hook and 2 strands A, work 1 row sc evenly around right front, back neck and left front edge. Do not turn. Work 1 row backwards sc (from left to right) in each sc. Sew zipper to fronts. Set in sleeves. Sew side and sleeve seams. With single strand F, embroider bullion st for feet and beak foll chart for placement.

BULLION STITCH

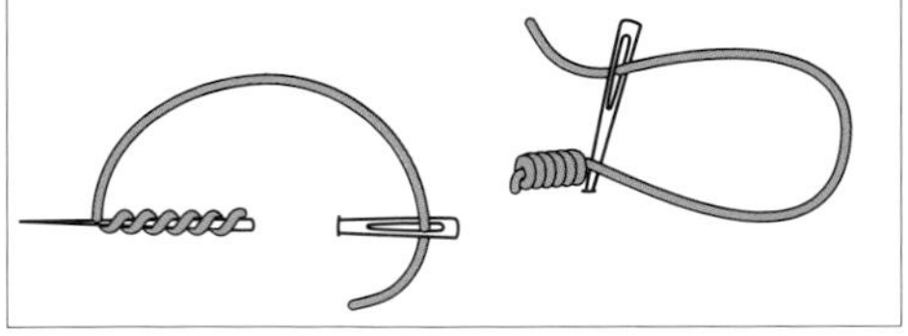

BOY'S CHART 2

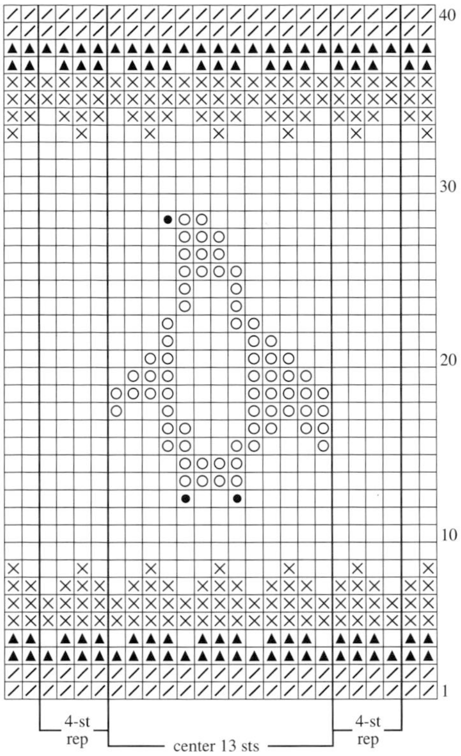

40
30
20
10
1
4-st rep
center 13 sts
4-st rep

Color Key

- ☒ Blue (A)
- ☐ White (B)
- ⊡ Black (C)
- ▲ Red (D)
- ⧄ Teal (E)
- ● Bullion St with yellow (F)

GIRL'S CHART 2

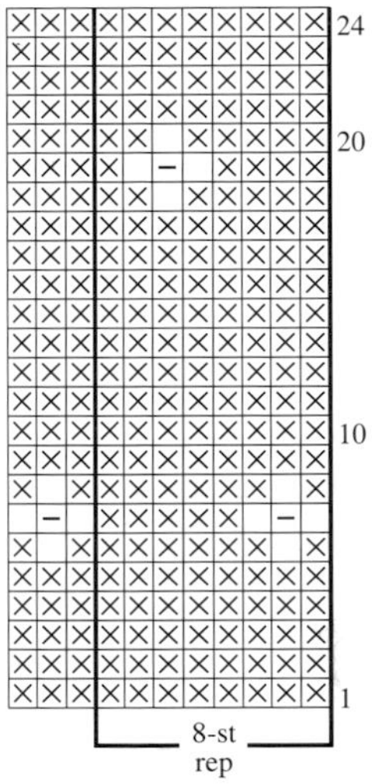

24
20
10
1
8-st rep

BOY'S CHART 1

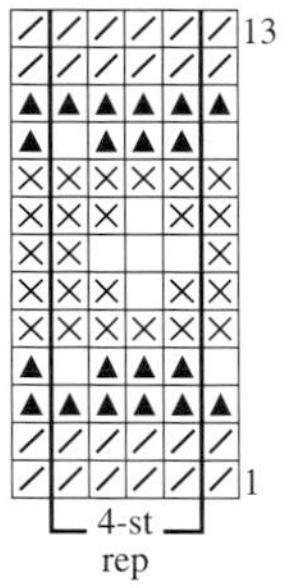

13
1
4-st rep

GIRL'S CHART 1

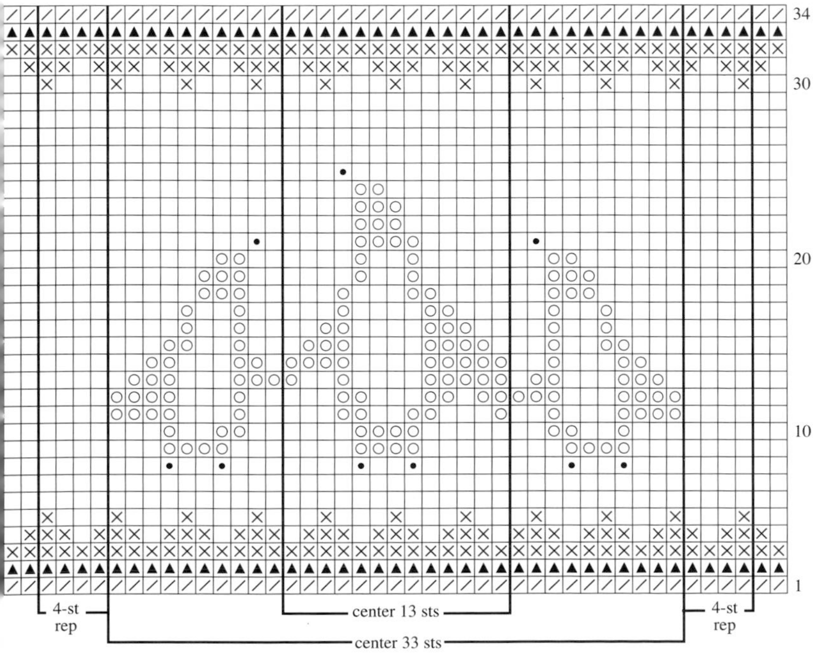

34
30
20
10
1
4-st rep
center 13 sts
center 33 sts
4-st rep

BOY'S SWEATER

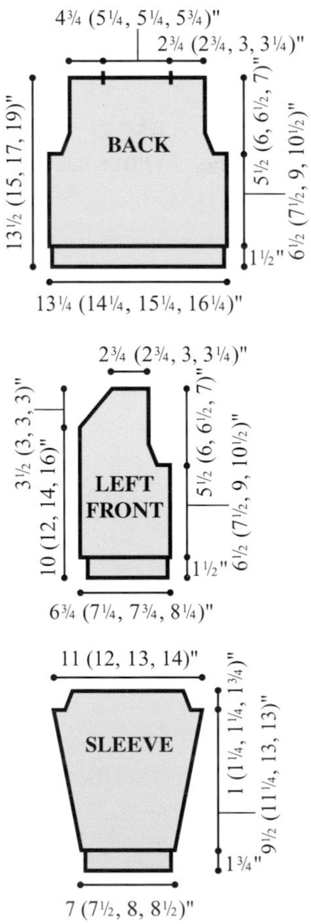

4¾ (5¼, 5¼, 5¾)"
2¾ (2¾, 3, 3¼)"
BACK
13½ (15, 17, 19)"
5½ (6, 6½, 7)"
6½ (7½, 9, 10½)"
1½"
13¼ (14¼, 15¼, 16¼)"
2¾ (2¾, 3, 3¼)"
LEFT FRONT
3½ (3, 3, 3)"
10 (12, 14, 16)"
5½ (6, 6½, 7)"
6½ (7½, 9, 10½)"
1½"
6¾ (7¼, 7¾, 8¼)"
11 (12, 13, 14)"
SLEEVE
1 (1¼, 1¼, 1¾)"
9½ (11¼, 13, 13)"
1¾"
7 (7½, 8, 8½)"

GIRL'S SWEATER

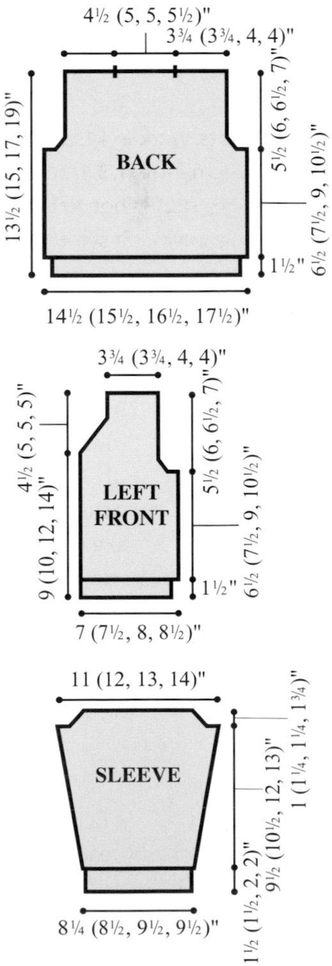

4½ (5, 5, 5½)"
3¾ (3¾, 4, 4)"
BACK
13½ (15, 17, 19)"
5½ (6, 6½, 7)"
6½ (7½, 9, 10½)"
1½"
14½ (15½, 16½, 17½)"
3¾ (3¾, 4, 4)"
LEFT FRONT
4½ (5, 5, 5)"
9 (10, 12, 14)"
5½ (6, 6½, 7)"
6½ (7½, 9, 10½)"
1½"
7 (7½, 8, 8½)"
11 (12, 13, 14)"
SLEEVE
1 (1¼, 1¼, 1¾)"
9½ (10½, 12, 13)"
1½ (1½, 2, 2)"
8¼ (8½, 9½, 9½)"

Two of a Kind
for intermediate knitters

Melissa Leapman's comfy zip-front pullovers update a traditional snowflake pattern in contemporary colors. Hers is done in a pretty violet and green mix; his in rugged blue and dark green. "Two of a Kind" first appeared in the Winter '98/'99 issue of *Family Circle Easy Knitting* magazine.

MATERIALS

Girl's version
- *Country Garden DK* by Patons®, 1³/₄oz/50g balls, each approx 135yd/125m (wool).
  4 (4, 5, 6, 6) balls in #38 lt green (A) and 2 (3, 4, 4, 5) balls in #28 violet (B)

Boy's version
  4 (4, 5, 6, 6) balls in #32 lt blue (A) and 2 (3, 4, 4, 5) balls in #43 dk green (B)
- One pair each sizes 5 and 6 (3.75 and 4mm) needles OR SIZE TO OBTAIN GAUGE
- Size 5 (3.75mm) circular needle, 16"/40cm long
- 7"/18cm zipper
- Sewing thread to match zipper
- Stitch holders

SIZES

Sized for Child's 4 (6, 8, 10, 12). Shown in sizes 4 and 6.

FINISHED MEASUREMENTS

- Chest 32 (34, 36, 38, 40)"/81 (86, 91.5, 96.5, 101.5)cm
- Length 17¹/₂ (18¹/₂, 19¹/₂, 21, 22¹/₂)"/44.5 (47, 49.5, 53, 57)cm
- Upper arm 12¹/₂ (13¹/₂, 14¹/₂, 15¹/₂, 16¹/₂)"/32 (34, 37, 39.5, 42)cm

GAUGE

24 sts and 28 rows to 4"/10cm over St st using larger needles.
TAKE TIME TO CHECK YOUR GAUGE.

BACK

With smaller needles and A, cast on 97 (103, 109, 115, 121) sts. Work in k1, p1 rib for 2"/5cm. Change to larger needles and cont in St st until piece measures 8 (8¹/₂, 9, 10, 11)"/20.5 (21.5, 23, 25.5, 28)cm from beg.

Beg chart

Row 1 (RS) Beg as indicated for chosen size, work row 1 foll chart to rep line, work 24-st rep 3 (3, 3, 4, 4) times, end as indicated for size. Cont to foll chart in this way through row 18. Piece measures approx 10¹/₂ (11, 11¹/₂, 12¹/₂, 13¹/₂)"/26.5 (28, 29, 32, 34)cm from beg.

Armhole shaping

Bind off 4 sts at beg of next 2 rows. **Next dec row (RS)** K1, ssk, work to last 3 sts, k2tog, k1. P1 row. **Note** Change to B after chart is completed. Rep last 2 rows 17 (18, 22, 23, 25) times. [**Next row (RS)** Rep dec row 1. **Dec row 2 (WS)** P1, p2tog tbl, work to last 3 sts, p2tog, p1] 5 (6, 5, 6, 6) times. Sl rem 33 (33, 35, 35, 37) sts to a holder for back neck.

FRONT

Work as for back, including beg of armhole shaping, until piece measures 10¹/₂ (11¹/₂, 12¹/₂, 14, 15¹/₂)"/26.5 (29, 32, 35.5, 39.5) cm from beg.

Beg placket opening

Next row (RS) Work to center 3 sts, sl these 3 sts to a safety pin for neck opening, join a 2nd ball of yarn and work to end. Cont to work both sides at once with separate balls of yarn, until piece measures 15¹/₂ (16, 17¹/₂, 19, 20¹/₂)"/39 (41.5, 44.5, 48, 52)cm from beg.

Neck shaping

From each neck edge, bind off 4 (4, 5, 5, 5) sts once, 3 sts once, 2 sts 3 times, dec 1 st every other row 2 (2, 2, 2, 3) times.

SLEEVES

With smaller needles and A, cast on 45 (45, 45, 47, 49) sts. Work in k2, p2 rib for 2"/5cm. Change to larger needles and cont in St st, inc 1 st each side every 2nd row 8 (10, 12, 13, 14) times, then every 4th row 7 (8, 9, 10, 11) times, AT SAME TIME, when piece measures 8 (9, 10, 11, 12¹/₂)"/20.5 (23, 25.5, 28, 31.5)cm from beg, beg chart by centering chart as indicated on center st, and cont to foll chart through row 18. There are 75 (81, 87, 93, 99) sts and piece measures 10¹/₂ (11¹/₂, 12¹/₂, 13¹/₂, 15)"/26.5 (29, 32, 34, 38)cm from beg.

Raglan cap shaping

Bind off 4 sts at beg of next 2 rows. Work dec row 1 (from back armhole) every other row 17 (18, 21, 22, 23) times then every row 12 (14, 14, 16, 18) times. Sl rem 9 sts to a holder.

FINISHING

Block pieces to measurements. Sew raglan seams.

Neckband

With circular needle and B, pick up and k 87 (87, 91, 91, 95) sts evenly around neck, including sts from holders. Work back and forth in k1, p1 rib

(Continued on page 133)

Game Night
for beginner knitters

Graphic pullovers in bold black and white are perfect for playtime. Designed by Mari Lynn Patrick, hers showcases a single star and striped edging; his features bold stripes across the body and sleeves. "Game Night" first appeared in the Winter '00/'01 issue of *Family Circle Easy Knitting* magazine

MATERIALS

Girl's sweater

- *Butterfly* by Filatura Di Crosa/Tahki•Stacy Charles, Inc., 1³/₄oz/50g balls each approx 192yd/175m (mohair/acrylic)
- 3 (4, 4) balls in #403 black (MC) and 1 ball in #400 white (CC)
- One pair each sizes 6 and 7 (4 and 4.5mm) needles OR SIZE TO OBTAIN GAUGE
- Size E (3.5mm) crochet hook
- Two ½"/13mm buttons

Boy's sweater

- *10-Ply* by Wool Pak Yarns NZ/Baabajoes Wool Co., 8½oz/250g hanks, each approx 430yd/396m (wool)
  2 (2, 2, 3) hanks in #01 ecru (MC) and 1 hank in #10 black (CC)
- One pair each sizes 6 and 8 (4 and 5mm) needles OR SIZE TO OBTAIN GAUGE
- Size 6 (4mm) circular needle, 16"/40cm long

SIZES

Girl's sweater

Sized for Child's 2 (4, 6). Shown in size 6.

Boy's sweater

Sized for Child's 4 (6, 8, 10). Shown in size 8.

FINISHED MEASUREMENTS

Girl's sweater

- Chest 28½ (30, 32)"/72.5 (76, 81)cm
- Length 14 (15, 16)"/35.5 (38, 40.5)cm
- Upper arm 10½ (11¼, 12)"/26.5 (28.5, 30.5)cm

Boy's sweater

- Chest 31 (33, 35, 38)"/78.5 (84, 87, 76.5)cm
- Length 15 (16½, 18, 19½)"/38 (42, 45.5, 50)cm
- Upper arm 11½ (12½, 13, 13³/₄)"/29 (32, 33, 35)cm

GAUGES

Girl's sweater

- 20 sts and 28 rows to 4"/10cm over St st using larger needles.

Boy's sweater

- 18 sts and 24 rows to 4"/10cm over St st using larger needles.

TAKE TIME TO CHECK YOUR GAUGE.

GIRL'S SWEATER

BACK

With smaller needles and CC, cast on 86 (90, 94) sts. **Row 1 (WS)** Purl. **Row 2** (picot turning ridge) K1, *k2tog, yo; rep from *, end k1. **Row 3** Purl. **Row 4 (RS)** Change to larger needles and MC, knit. With MC, k 1 row, p 2 rows. **Row 8 (RS)** K2 with CC, *k2 with MC, k2 with CC; rep from * to end. **Row 9** P2 with MC, *p2 with CC, p2 with MC; rep from * to end. K 1 row with MC. K 1 row (on WS) with MC. P 1 row with MC, dec 1 st at end of row—85 (89, 93) sts. Beg with a p row, cont in St st, dec 1 st each side every 6th (8th, 8th) row 7 times—71 (75, 79) sts. Work even until piece measures 9 (9½, 10)"/23 (24, 25.5)cm above picot turning ridge.

Armhole shaping

Bind off 4 sts at beg of next 2 rows. Dec 1 st each side of next row then every other row twice more—57 (61, 65) sts. Work even until armhole measures 5 (5½, 6)"/12.5 (14, 15)cm. Bind off.

FRONT

Work as for back until piece measures 6 (6½,

7)"/15 (16.5, 18)cm above picot turning ridge.

Beg star chart

Mark center 29 sts and work these center marked sts foll star chart and rem sts with MC, through row 31, then cont with MC only, and AT SAME TIME, cont side seam decs and armhole shaping as on back until armhole measures 2½ (3, 3½)"/6.5 (7.5, 9)cm.

Neck shaping

Next row (RS) K24 (25, 27), join another ball of yarn and bind off center 9 (11, 11) sts, k to end. Working both sides at once, bind off 2 sts from each neck edge 3 times, dec 1 st every other row twice. When same length as back, bind off rem 16 (17, 19) sts each side for shoulders.

SLEEVES

With smaller needles and CC, cast on 38 sts. Work in edge pat for 12 rows as on back (only do not dec on last row). Then cont in St st with MC inc 1 st each side every 4th row 0 (2, 5) times, every 6th row 7 (7, 6) times—52 (56, 60) sts. Work even until piece measures 8½ (10½, 11½)"/21.5 (26.5, 29)cm above picot turning ridge.

Cap shaping

Bind off 4 sts at beg of next 2 rows, 3 sts at beg of next 2 rows, 2 sts at beg of next 10 rows. Bind off rem 18 (22, 26) sts.

FINISHING

Block pieces to measurements. Sew right shoulder seam.

Neckband

With smaller needles and MC, pick up and k 60 (64, 64) sts around neck edge. [P 1, row, k 1 row], twice. Bind off purlwise. Beg at shoulder edge, sew left shoulder seam leaving last 2½"/6.5cm from neck edge open (including rolled neckband). With crochet hook, work an edge of sc around open neck edge (including neckband). Ch 5, (buttonloop), turn, skip 2 sc and sl st in each sc to 2 sc before shoulder, ch 5, sl st in each sc to end. Fasten off. Sew buttons to back opposite buttonloops. Turn up picot hems to WS and sew in place. Sew sleeves into armholes. Sew side and sleeve seams.

BOY'S SWEATER

BACK

With smaller needles and CC, cast on 69 (75, 79, 85) sts. K 1 row, p 1 row. Change to larger needles and MC and beg with a purl (WS) row, work in St st until piece measures 9½ (10½, 11½, 12½)"/24 (27, 29, 32)cm from beg.

Armhole shaping

Next (dec) row (RS) K2, k2tog, k to last 4 sts, SKP, k2. Rep dec row every other row 4 (4, 5, 6) times more—59 (65, 67, 71) sts. Work even until armhole measures 5½ (6, 6½, 7)"/14 (15, 16.5, 18)cm. Bind off.

FRONT

Work as for back until piece measures 6½ (7½, 8½, 9½)"/16.5 (19.5, 21.5, 24.5)cm from beg.

Beg stripe pat

Row 1 (RS) With MC, k 24 (26, 27, 30), with CC k 45 (49, 52, 55). Cont stripe pat working 9 more rows as established, then work 7 rows with MC; rep between *'s once (27 rows in total for stripe pat), AT SAME TIME, when same length as back, shape armholes as on back—59 (65, 67, 71) sts. Work even with MC until armhole measures 1¾ (2, 2½, 3)"/4.5 (5, 6.5, 7.5)cm.

V-neck shaping

Next row (RS) K29 (32, 33, 35), join another ball of yarn and bind off center st, k to end. Working both sides at once, dec 1 st each side of neck every 4th row once, every 6th row once. Work even until V-neck measures 2¼ (2½, 2½, 2½)"/6 (6.5, 6.5, 6.5)cm.

Neck shaping

Bind off from each neck edge 4 sts once, 2 (2, 3, 3) sts once, dec 1 st each side every other row twice—19 (22, 22, 24) sts rem each side. When same length as back, bind off rem sts each side for shoulders.

LEFT SLEEVE

With smaller needles and CC, cast on 30 (32, 32, 34) sts. K 1 row, p 1 row. Change to larger needles and MC and beg with a purl (WS) row, work in St st, inc 1 st each side every alternate 4th and 6th rows a total of 11 (12, 13, 14) times and AT SAME TIME, when piece measures 4 (4½, 5, 6)"/10 (11.5, 13, 15)cm from beg, work stripe pat as foll: **Next row (RS)** With CC, k 27 (29, 30, 32), with MC, k to end. Cont in stripe pat over 27 rows total as on front and when all incs are completed, work even on 52 (56, 58, 62) sts until piece measures 9½ (10½, 11½, 12½)"/24 (26.5, 29, 31.5)cm from beg.

Cap shaping

Work as for back armhole shaping—42 (46, 46, 48) sts. Bind off.

RIGHT SLEEVE

Work as for left sleeve, working CC stripe at end of RS rows.

FINISHING

Block pieces to measurements. Sew shoulder seams.

Neck trim

With circular needles and CC, working in back lps of sts only, pick up and k 22 (22, 24, 24) sts along back neck, 15 (15, 16, 16) sts around front neck shaping, pm, *12 (13, 13, 13) sts along side of V-point, pm; rep from * once, 15 (15, 16, 16) sts around front neck shaping—76 (78, 82, 82) sts. Then bind off all sts purlwise while inc 1 st each side of markers at top of neck and p3tog at center of V-neck. Sew sleeves into armholes. Sew side and sleeve seams.

BOY'S SWEATER

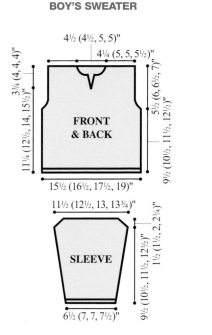

4½ (4½, 5, 5)"

4¼ (5, 5, 5½)"

3¾ (4, 4, 4)"

11¼ (12½, 14, 15½)"

FRONT & BACK

5½ (6, 6½, 7)"

9½ (10½, 11½, 12½)"

15½ (16½, 17½, 19)"

11½ (12½, 13, 13¾)"

SLEEVE

1½ (1½, 2, 2¼)"

9½ (10½, 11½, 12½)"

6½ (7, 7, 7½)"

GIRL'S SWEATER

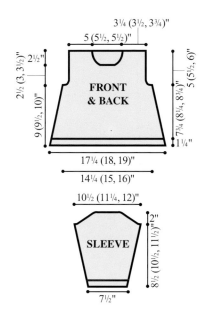

3¼ (3½, 3¾)"

5 (5½, 5½)"

2½"

2½ (3, 3½)"

9 (9½, 10)"

FRONT & BACK

5 (5½, 6)"

7¾ (8¼, 8¾)"

1¼"

17¼ (18, 19)"

14¼ (15, 16)"

10½ (11¼, 12)"

SLEEVE

2"

8½ (10½, 11½)"

7½"

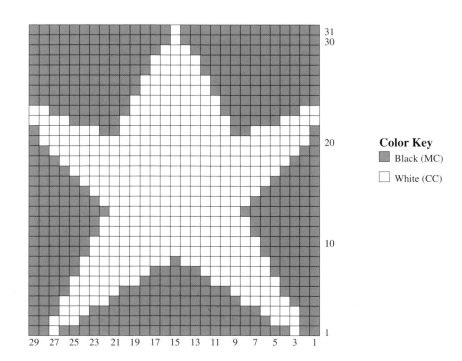

31
30

20

10

1

29 27 25 23 21 19 17 15 13 11 9 7 5 3 1

Color Key

▦ Black (MC)

☐ White (CC)

Blue Note
for beginner knitters

Crunchy texture on a classic silhouette lends a modern edge as well as casual comfort to Melissa Leapman's rugged turtleneck. Quick and easy to knit, "Blue Note" first appeared in the Fall '01 issue of *Family Circle Easy Knitting* magazine.

MATERIALS
- *Wool Ease Chunky* by Lion Brand Yarns Co., 5oz/140g balls, each approx 153yd/141m (acrylic/wool)
  5 (6, 7, 7) balls in #115 blue
- One pair each sizes 10½ (6.5mm) needles OR SIZE TO OBTAIN GAUGE
- One each sizes 10½ (6.5mm) circular needle, 16"/40cm long
- Stitch holders

SIZES
Sized for Child's 8 (10, 12, 14). Shown in size 12.

FINISHED MEASUREMENTS
- Chest 34 (36½, 39, 42)"/86 (92.5, 99. 106.5)cm
- Length 17½ (18½, 20, 21½)"/44.5 (47, 51, 54.5)cm
- Upper arm 14 (15, 16, 17)"/35.5 (38, 41, 43)cm

GAUGE
13 sts and 26 rows to 4"/10cm over fisherman's rib pat using size 10½ (6.5mm) needles.
TAKE TIME TO CHECK YOUR GAUGE.

FISHERMAN'S RIB PATTERN
(over an odd no. of sts)
Row 1 Knit.
Row 2 P1, *k1 st in the center of the st in the row below st on needle (k1-6), p1; rep from * to end.
Rep these 2 rows for fisherman's rib pat.
Note
Selvage sts at beg and end of rows do not count in the finished measurements.

BACK
With size 10½ (6.5mm) needles, cast on 57 (61, 65, 69) sts. Work in fisherman's rib pat until piece measures 10½ (11, 12, 13)"/26.5 (28, 30.5, 33)cm from beg.
Armhole shaping
Bind off 4 sts at beg of next 2 rows—49 (53, 57, 61) sts. Work even until armhole measures 7 (7½, 8, 8½)"/18 (19, 20.5, 21.5)cm. Bind off.

FRONT
Work as for back until armhole measures 5 (5½, 6, 6½)"/12.5 (14, 15, 16.5)cm.
Neck shaping
Next row (RS) Work 21 (23, 24, 26) sts, join a 2nd ball of yarn and bind off center 7 (7, 9, 9) sts, work to end. Working both sides at once, bind off 2 sts from each neck edge twice, dec 1 st every other row 3 times—14 (16, 17, 19) sts rem each side. When same length as back, bind off sts each side for shoulders.

SLEEVES
With size 10½ (6.5mm) needles, cast on 29 (31, 33, 33) sts. Work in fisherman's rib pat inc 1 st each side every 8th row 1 (0, 1, 2) times, every 10th row 8 (8, 10, 10) times, every 12th row 0 (2, 0, 0) times—47 (51, 55, 57) sts. Work even until piece measures 14¾ (17, 17¾, 19)"/37.5 (43, 45, 48)cm from beg. Bind off.

FINISHING
Block pieces to measurements. Sew shoulder seams.
Turtleneck
With smaller circular needle, pick up and k 58 (58, 62, 62) sts evenly around neck edge. Join and work in rnds of k1, p1 rib for 2½"/6.5cm.

Change to larger circular needle and cont until turtleneck measures 5"/13cm. Bind off loosely in rib. Sew sleeves into armholes. Sew side and sleeve seams.

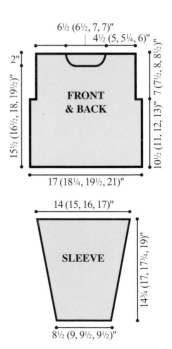

6½ (6½, 7, 7)"
4½ (5, 5¼, 6)"
2"
15½ (16½, 18, 19½)"
FRONT & BACK
7 (7½, 8, 8½)"
10½ (11, 12, 13)"
17 (18¼, 19½, 21)"

14 (15, 16, 17)"
SLEEVE
14¾ (17, 17¾, 19)"
8½ (9, 9½, 9½)"

Chill Out

for beginner knitters

Skiing, snowboarding, skating or just kicking back, he'll cut a fine figure in this sporty turtleneck. Featuring ribbed cuffs and bold orange and yellow bands, it knits up quick. "Chill Out" first appeared in the Fall '00 issue of *Family Circle Easy Knitting* magazine.

MATERIALS

■ *Tenerezza* by Lane Borgosesia, 1³/₄oz/50g balls, each approx 147yd/135m (wool/acrylic)

3 skeins each in #3793 red (A) and #25536 royal (C)

12 (13, 14) balls in #11 black (MC)

1 ball each in #25572 orange (A) and #18 yellow (B)

■ One pair each sizes 3 and 4 (3 and 3.5mm) needles OR SIZE TO OBTAIN GAUGE

■ Size 3 (3mm) circular needle, 16"/40cm long

SIZES

Sized for Child's 12 (14, 16). Shown in size 12.

FINISHED MEASUREMENTS

■ Chest 42 (45, 48)"/106.5 (114, 122)cm

■ Length 24 (25½, 27)"/61 (64.5, 68.5)cm

■ Upperarm 20 (21, 22)"/51 (53, 56)cm

GAUGE

23 sts and 32 rows to 4"/10cm over St st using larger needles.

TAKE TIME TO CHECK YOUR GAUGE.

STRIPE PATTERN

3 rows B, 6 rows A, 2 rows MC, 2 rows B, 7 rows MC, 2 rows B, 2 rows MC, 2 rows A, 2 rows MC, 2 rows B, 7 rows MC, 2 rows B, 6 rows A, 3 rows B.

BACK

With smaller needles and MC, cast on 122 (130, 138) sts. Work in k2, p2 rib for 2"/5cm. Change to larger needles and work in St st until piece measures 11½ (12¼, 13)"/29 (31, 33)cm from beg. Work 48 rows stripe pat. Cont with MC only until piece measures 24 (25½, 27)"/61 (64.5, 68.5)cm from beg. Bind off all sts.

FRONT

Work as for back until piece measures 22 (23½, 25)"/56 (59.5, 63.5)cm from beg, end with a WS row.

Neck shaping

Next row (RS) Work 53 (56, 60) sts, join 2nd ball of yarn and bind off center 16 (18, 18) sts, work to end. Working both sides at once, bind off from each neck edge 4 sts once, 3 sts once, 2 sts twice, 1 st once. When same length as back, bind off rem 41 (44, 48) sts each side for shoulders.

SLEEVES

With smaller needles and MC, cast on 64 (66, 68) sts. Work in k2, p2 rib for 2"/5cm. Change to larger needles and work in St st, inc 1 st each side every 4th row 20 (21, 23) times, every 6th row 6 times—116 (120, 126) sts. Work even until piece measures 17½ (18, 19)"/44 (45.5, 48)cm from beg. Bind off all sts.

FINISHING

Block pieces to measurements. Sew shoulder seams.

Turtleneck

With RS facing, circular needle and MC, pick up and k 92 (96, 96) sts evenly around neck edge. Join and work in k2, p2 rib for 6½"/16cm. Bind off in rib. Place markers 10 (10½, 11)"/25.5 (26.5, 28)cm down from shoulders on front and back. Sew top of sleeve between markers. Sew side and sleeve seams.

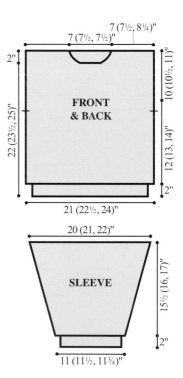

Summer Fun

Wee ones beat the heat with snazzy knits in jazzy colors.

Happy Campers

This colorful pair packs along the comforts of home. His roomy pullover incorporates a clever front pocket with ribbed openings at the side; her hooded sweatshirt sports a zip placket and garter-stitched envelope flap. Both are designed by Lila P. Chin. (Instructions for matching socks appear on page 100.) "Happy Campers" first appeared in the Spring/Summer '98 issue of *Family Circle Easy Knitting* magazine.

MATERIALS

Boy's Sweater
- *Sand* by Classic Elite Yarns, 3½oz/100g hanks, each approx 154yd/140m (cotton)
  2 (3, 3, 4, 4) hanks in #6435 green (A)
  2 (2, 2, 3, 3) hanks in #6404 turquoise (B)
- One pair each sizes 5 and 7 (3.75 and 4.5mm) needles OR SIZE TO OBTAIN GAUGE
- One extra size 7 (4.5mm) needle for pocket
- Size 5 (3.75mm) circular needle, 16"/40cm long
- Stitch holder and stitch marker

Girl's Sweater
- *Cotton Fleece* by Brown Sheep Co., 3½oz/l00g balls, each approx 215yd/197m (cotton/wool)
  3 (4, 4, 5, 6) balls in #CW340 goldenrod (MC)
  3 (3, 3, 4, 4) balls #CW310 orange (CC)
- One pair each sizes 5 and 6 (3.75 and 4mm) needles OR SIZE TO OBTAIN GAUGE
- 4"/10cm matching zipper
- One button

SIZES

Both Sweaters
Sized for Child's 2 (4, 6, 8, 10). Shown in size 6.

FINISHED MEASUREMENTS

Boy's Sweater
- Chest 30 (32, 34, 36, 38)"/75 (80, 85, 90, 95)cm
- Length 14½ (16, 18, 19, 20½)"/36.5 (40.5, 45.5, 48, 52)cm
- Upper arm 12 (13, 14, 15, 16)"/30 (33, 35, 38, 40)cm

Girl's Sweater
- Chest 30 (32, 34, 36, 38)"/75 (80, 85, 90, 95)cm
- Length 14½ (16, 18, 19, 20½)"/36.5 (40.5, 45.5, 48, 52)cm
- Upper arm 12 (13, 14, 15, 16)"/30 (33, 35, 38, 40)cm

GAUGES

Boy's Sweater
- 16 sts and 24 rows to 4"/10cm over St st using larger needles.

Girl's Sweater
- 20 sts and 28 rows to 4"/10cm over St st using larger needles.

TAKE TIME TO CHECK YOUR GAUGE.

STITCHES USED

Stripe Pattern
6 rows B, 12 rows A; rep from * (18 rows) for stripe pat.

BOY'S SWEATER

BACK

With smaller needles and B, cast on 61 (65, 69, 73, 77) sts. Work in k1, p1 rib for 1"/2.5cm, dec 1 st on last row—60 (64, 68, 72, 76) sts. Change to larger needles and A. Work in St st until piece measures 5½ (6, 7, 8, 8½)"/14 (15.5, 18, 20.5, 22)cm from beg, end with a WS row. Cont in St st and stripe pat until piece measures 1½ (16, 18, 19, 20½)"/36.5 (40.5, 45.5, 48, 52)cm from beg, end with 12 rows A (6 rows B, 6 rows A, 6 rows A, 12 rows A). Bind off all sts with A (B, A, A, A).

FRONT

Pocket lining
With larger needles and A, cast on 40 (44, 46, 48, 50) sts. Work in St st for 4½ (5, 6, 7, 7½)"/11.5 (13, 15.5, 18, 19)cm. Place sts on a holder. Work as for back until rib is complete.

Pocket opening
Next row (RS) Work 11 (11, 12, 13, 14) sts, join 2nd ball of yarn and work 38 (42, 44, 46, 48) sts, join 3rd ball of yarn and work to end. Cont to work all three sections at same time with separate balls, until piece measures 5½ (6, 7, 8, 8½)"/14 (15.5, 18, 20.5, 22)cm from beg, end with a WS row.

Pocket joining
Next row (RS) With B, k 10 (10, 11, 12, 13), sl lining sts to a 3rd size 7 needle so that K sts are facing you, hold these sts to back of work, *k

next st on LH needle tog with first st on 3rd needle; rep from * until all lining sts have been worked, work to end. Cut extra balls of yarn and work with one ball only until 18 (24, 24, 24, 30) rows of stripe pat have been worked—piece measures $8\frac{1}{2}$ (10, 11, 12, $13\frac{1}{2}$)"/21.5 (25.5, 28, 30.5, 34)cm from beg.

Placket shaping

Next row (RS) Work 28 (30, 31, 33, 35) sts, join 2nd ball of yarn and bind off center 4 (4, 6, 6, 6) sts, work to end. Cont in stripe pat and work both sides at once until piece measures $12\frac{1}{2}$ (14, 16, 17, $18\frac{1}{2}$)"/31.5 (35.5, 40.5, 43, 46.5)cm from beg.

Neck shaping

Next row (RS) Bind off from each neck edge 4 sts once, 2 sts twice, 1 st twice. Work even until same length as back. Bind off rem 18 (20, 21, 23, 25) sts each side for shoulders.

SLEEVES

With smaller needles and B, cast on 27 (29, 29, 31, 33) sts. Work in k1, p1 rib for 1"/2.5cm, inc 1 st on last row—28 (30, 30, 32, 34) sts. Change to larger needles and A. Work in St st and stripe pat (beg with 12 rows A) until 54 rows have been worked, ending with 6 rows B, then cont with A to end of piece, AT SAME TIME, inc 1 st each side every 4th row 6 (4, 8, 7, 6) times, every 6th row 4 (7, 5, 7, 9) times—8 (52, 56, 60, 64) sts. Work even until piece measures 10 ($11\frac{1}{2}$, $12\frac{1}{2}$, $13\frac{1}{2}$, 15)"/25.5 (29, 32, 34, 38)cm from beg. Bind off all sts.

FINISHING

Pocket bands

With RS facing, smaller needles and B, pick up and k sts evenly along each side of pocket. Work in k1, p1 rib for 1"/2.5cm. Bind off in rib. Sew shoulder seams. Place markers 6 ($6\frac{1}{2}$, 7, $7\frac{1}{2}$, 8)"/15 (16.5, 17.5, 19, 20)cm down from shoulder seams on fronts and back for armholes. Sew top of sleeve to front and back between markers. Sew side and sleeve seams.

Neckband

Place marker at center back neck. With RS facing,

circular needle and B, pick up and k 7 sts on each side of marker—14 sts. Work in k1, p1 rib for 1 row. Cont in rib, picking up 3 sts around neck at beg of next 12 (12, 14, 14, 14) rows—50 (50, 56, 56, 56) sts. **Next row (RS)** Pick up and k 19 (19, 24, 24, 24) sts along right front placket, rib 50 (50, 56, 56, 56) sts, pick up and k 19 (19, 24, 24, 24) sts along left front placket. Cont in rib for 1 (1, $1\frac{1}{2}$, $1\frac{1}{2}$, $1\frac{1}{2}$)"/2.5 (2.5, 4, 4, 4)cm. Bind off in rib. Sew ends of band, right over left, along center front bound-off sts.

GIRL'S SWEATER

BACK

With smaller needles and CC, cast on 75 (80, 86, 90, 95) sts. Work in garter st for 1 (1, $1\frac{1}{2}$, $1\frac{1}{2}$, $1\frac{1}{2}$)"/2.5 (2, 5, 4, 4, 4)cm. Change to larger needles and MC. Work in St st until piece measures $14\frac{1}{2}$ (16, 18, 19, $20\frac{1}{2}$)"/36.5 (40.5, 45.5, 48, 52)cm from beg. Bind off all sts.

FRONT

Work as for back until piece measures 9 ($10\frac{1}{2}$, 12, 13, $14\frac{1}{2}$)"/22.5 (26.5, 30.5, 33, 37)cm from beg, end with a WS row.

Placket shaping

Next row (RS) Work 35 (37, 40, 42, 44) sts, join 2nd ball of yarn and bind off center 5 (6, 6, 6, 7) sts, work to end. Cont working both sides at once until placket measures 4"/10cm, end with a WS row.

Neck shaping

Next row (RS) Bind off from each neck edge 5 sts once, 3 sts once, 2 sts twice, 1 st 1 (1, 2, 2, 2) times. Work even until same length as back. Bind off rem 22 (24, 26, 28, 30) sts each side for shoulder.

SLEEVES

With smaller needles and CC, cast on 34 (35, 38, 39, 40) sts. Work in garter st for 1 (1, $1\frac{1}{2}$, $1\frac{1}{2}$, $1\frac{1}{2}$)"/2.5 (2.5, 4, 4, 4)cm. Change to larger needles and MC. Work in St st, inc 1 st each side every 4th row 13 (15, 16, 18, 20) times—60 (65, 70, 75, 80) sts. Work even until piece measures 10 ($11\frac{1}{2}$, $12\frac{1}{2}$, $13\frac{1}{2}$, 15)"/25.5 (29, 32, 34, 38)cm from beg. Bind off all sts.

HOOD - LEFT HALF

With larger needles and CC, cast on 33 (35, 38, 38, 38) sts. Work in St st for 9 (10, $10\frac{1}{2}$, $11\frac{1}{2}$, $12\frac{1}{2}$)"/23 (25,5, 26.5, 29, 32)cm, end with a WS row.

Top shaping

Bind off at beg of RS rows: 8 (8, 7, 7, 7) sts 3 (1, 2, 2, 2) times, 9 (9, 8, 8, 8) sts 1 (3, 3, 3, 3) times. Work right half of hood to correspond, reversing top shaping.

POCKET

With larger needles and MC, cast on 44 (46, 48, 48, 50) sts. Work in St st and stripes as foll: *2 rows MC, 1 row CC, 2 rows MC, 6 rows CC; rep from * (11 rows) for stripes until piece measures 6 ($6\frac{1}{2}$, 7, 7, $7\frac{1}{2}$)"/15 (16.5, 17.5, 17.5, 19)cm. Bind off all sts.

Pocket flap

With smaller needles and CC, cast on 12 (12, 14, 14, 14) sts. Work in garter st, inc 1 st at beg of every row, until piece measures 1 (1, $1\frac{1}{4}$, $1\frac{1}{4}$, $1\frac{1}{4}$)"/2.5 (2.5, 3, 3, 3)cm, end with a WS row. On next row, work to center 2 sts, yo, k2tog for buttonhole, work to end. Cont to work inc's as before until there are 44 (46, 48, 48, 50) sts. Work even for 1"/2.5cm. Bind off.

FINISHING

Place pocket at center front and sew in place. Place pocket flap $\frac{1}{4}$"/.5cm above pocket and sew in place. Sew button on pocket opposite buttonhole. Sew shoulder seams. Place markers 6 ($6\frac{1}{2}$, 7, $7\frac{1}{2}$, 8)"/15 (16.5, 17.5, 19, 20)cm down from shoulder seams on fronts and back for armholes. Sew top of sleeve to front and back between markers. Sew side and sleeve seams. Sew hood around neck and sew seam.

Placket and hood edging

With RS facing, smaller needles and CC, pick up and k 21 sts along right front placket, 53 (59, 62, 68, 74) sts along edge of hood, 21 sts along left front placket—95 (101, 104, 110, 116) sts. Work in garter st for $\frac{1}{4}$"/2cm. Bind off loosely. Sew front placket rib in place. Sew in zipper.

(See schematics on page 134)

Sunflower Girl

The outdoor life is more fun in Agi Revesz's sprightly sunflower-patch pullover. Accented with rolled edges, blanket stitching and crocheted buttons at shoulders, this meadow treasure deserves a green thumbs-up! "Sunflower Girl" first appeared in the Spring/Summer '98 issue of *Family Circle Easy Knitting* magazine.

MATERIALS

- *Cotton Classic* by Tahki Yarns 1¾oz/50g, each approx 108yd/100m (wool)
  6 (6, 7) hanks in #3726 kiwi (MC)
  1 (1, 2) hanks in #3861 navy (A)
  1 hank each in #3001 white (B), #3533 yellow (C) and #3402 orange (D)
- One pair each sizes 5 and 6 (3.75 and 4mm) knitting needles OR SIZE NEEDED TO OBTAIN GAUGE
- Size D/3 (3mm) crochet hook
- Two ¾"/2mm plastic rings

FINISHED MEASUREMENTS

- Chest 31 (35, 37)"/78 (88, 94)cm
- Length 16½ (18½, 20½)"/42 (47, 52)cm
- Upper arm 13½ (14, 15½)"/33 (35, 39)cm

GAUGE

20 sts and 28 rows to 4"/10cm over St st using larger needles.
TAKE TIME TO CHECK YOUR GAUGE.

Note

When working center block, work with a separate ball of yarn and twist yarns when changing colors to prevent holes.

BACK

With smaller needles and A, cast on 78 (88, 94) sts. Work in St st for 8 rows. Change to larger needles and MC and cont in St st until piece measures 16½ (18½, 20½)"/42 (47, 52)cm from beg (with edge rolled). Bind off.

FRONT

Work as for back until piece measures 7¾ (9¾, 11¾)"/19.5 (25, 30)cm from beg (with edge rolled). **Next row (RS)** With MC, k 28 (33, 36), with B, k22, join 2nd ball of MC and k28 (33, 36). Cont in colors as established for 33 more rows. Cut B and cont with MC only until piece measures 14½ (16½, 18½)"/37 (42, 47)cm from beg.

Neck shaping

Next row (RS) K35 (39, 40), join 2nd ball of MC and bind off center 8 (10, 14) sts, k to end. Working both sides at once, bind off from each neck edge 3 sts twice, 2 sts once, dec 1 st every other row twice. When same length as back, bind off rem 25 (29, 30) sts each side for shoulders.

SLEEVES

With smaller needles and A, cast on 36 (40, 42) sts. Work in St st for 8 rows. Change to larger needles and MC and cont in St st inc 1 st each side every 4th row 7 (5, 11) times, every 6th row 8 (10, 7) times—66 (70, 78) sts. Work even until piece measures 12½ (13½, 14½)"/32 (34, 37)cm from beg. Bind off.

FINISHING

Block pieces to measurements. Sew right shoulder seam. With smaller needles and A, pick up and k 70 (74, 82) sts evenly around neck edge. Work in St st for 6 rows. Bind off loosely.

Buttonhole band

With crochet hook and MC, work 1 sc in each st of front shoulder. Ch 1, turn. Next row Work 2 sc, ch 4, skip 4 sc (buttonhole), work 6 sc, work 2nd buttonhole, sc to end. Ch 1, turn. Next row Work 1 sc in each sc and 4 sc in each ch. Fasten off. Work back shoulder band in same way omitting buttonholes. Sew sleeves into armholes. Sew side and sleeve seams.

CENTER FLOWER

With crochet hook and D, beg at center, ch 5, join with sl st to form ring. **Rnd 1** Ch 3, [1 dc in ring, ch 1] 9 times, join with a sl st to 3rd ch of t-ch. **Rnd 2** Ch 3, dc in first ch-1 sp, [ch 1, dc, ch 1, dc in next ch-1 sp] 9 times, ch 1, pull D lp through top of t-ch, then pull C through 2 lps on hook. **Rnd 3** With C, ch 8, *sl st in 2nd ch from hook, sc in each of next 3 ch, htc in each ch to end, * skip next ch-1, dc and ch-1 and working into back lp only, sl st in back lp of next dc, ch 11, rep between *'s, sl st into back lp of next dc, ch 7, rep between *'s, sl st into back lp of next dc. Cont petals in this way by ch 10, then ch 11. Rep these 5 petals until there are a total of 19 petals. Join with sl st at beg. Fasten off. Pin flower to center square and sew in place.

Trim

With crochet hook and A, ch 121. **Rnd 1** 1 hdc in 2nd ch from hook and in next 28 ch, *3 hdc in next ch (corner), 1 hdc in next 29 ch; rep from * twice more, 3 hdc in corner. Join with a sl st and fasten off. Pin trim around center square and sew in place using B and blanket st. Work blanket st in same way around all edges.

(Continued on page 135)

Budding Beauty
for intermediate knitters

A tiny flowerpot accents the front of this classy cardigan. Simple reverse-stockinette stitchwork forms the flower motif; garter-stitch bands trimmed with tiny blossom buttons provide the perfect finishing touch. "Budding Beauty" first appeared in the Spring/Summer '00 issue of *Family Circle Easy Knitting* magazine.

MATERIALS
- *Summer* by Sesia/Lane Borgosesia, 1³/₄oz/50g balls, each approx 95yd/88m (cotton) 5 (6, 6, 7, 7, 8) balls in #56 peach OR #444 pink
- One pair size 6 (4mm) needles OR SIZE TO OBTAIN GAUGE
- Five ⁵/₈"/15mm buttons
- Stitch holders

SIZES
Sized for Child's 12 mo (18 mo, 2, 4, 6, 8). Shown in size 4.

FINISHED MEASUREMENTS
- Chest 24 (25¹/₂, 27, 29, 31, 33)"/61 (64.5, 68.5, 73.5, 78.5, 83.5)cm
- Length 11 (12, 12¹/₂, 13¹/₂, 14¹/₂, 16)"/28 (30.5, 31.5, 34, 37, 40.5)cm
- Upper arm 10 (11, 12, 12, 13, 14)"/25.5 (28, 30.5, 30.5, 33, 35.5)cm

GAUGE
20 sts and 28 rows to 4"/10cm over St st using size 6 (4mm) needles.
TAKE TIME TO CHECK YOUR GAUGE.

BACK
Cast on 60 (64, 68, 73, 78, 83) sts. Work in garter st for 1"/2.5cm. Cont in St st until piece measures 11 (12, 12¹/₂, 13¹/₂, 14¹/₂, 16)"/28 (30.5, 31.5, 34, 37, 40.5)cm from beg. Bind off all sts.

Left front
Cast on 33 (34, 37, 39, 43, 45) sts. Work in garter st for 1"/2.5cm, end with a RS row. **Next row (WS)** K 7 sts and place on holder, k to end. Work in St st for 1"/2.5cm.

Beg chart
For sizes 12 mo, 18 mo and 2
K9 (10, 11), work sts 1 to 8 of chart 1, k to end.

Work as established through row 29 of chart. Cont in St st until piece measures 9 (10, 10¹/₂)"/23 (25.5, 26.5)cm from beg. Beg neck shaping.
For sizes 4, 6 and 8
K10 (12, 13), work sts 1 to 12 of chart 2, k to end. Work as established through row 39 of chart. Cont in St st until piece measures 11¹/₂ (12¹/₂, 14)"/29 (31.5, 35.5)cm from beg. Beg neck shaping.

Neck shaping
Next row (WS) Bind off 4 (3, 4, 4, 5, 5) sts, work to end. Cont to bind off at neck edge 2 (2, 2, 2, 3, 4) sts once, then dec 1 st every other row 3 times. Bind off rem 17 (19, 21, 23, 25, 26) sts for shoulder.

Right front
Work to correspond to left front, reversing all shaping and placement of garter st band.

SLEEVES
Note Sizes 4, 6 and 8 have ³/₄-length sleeves. Cast on 30 (33, 36, 40, 43, 46) sts. Work in garter st for 1"/2.5cm. Work in St st, inc 1 st each side every other row 4 (1, 0, 0, 1, 0) times, then every 4th row 6 (10, 12, 10, 10, 12) times—50 (55, 60, 60, 65, 70) sts. Work even until piece measures 7¹/₂ (8, 9, 8, 8¹/₂, 9)"/19 (20.5, 23, 20.5, 21.5, 23)cm from beg. Bind off all sts.

FINISHING
Block pieces to measurements.
Collar
With WS facing, pick up and k 66 (70, 72, 73, 80, 88) sts around neck. **Next row (WS)** P3, work in garter st to last 3 sts, p3. Keeping the first and last 3 sts in St st, work in garter st for 2"/5cm. P 1 row, k 1 row, p 1 row. **Next row (WS)** P 1 row for turning ridge. Work 3 rows in St st. Bind off all sts. Turn hem to WS and sew in place.

Left front band
K7 sts from holder. Work in garter st until piece fits along front. Sew to edge. Place markers for buttons with the first one 1¹/₄"/3cm from the lower edge, the last one ¹/₂"/1.5cm from the top edge and the other 3 spaced evenly between.

Right front band
Work to correspond to left front band working buttonholes opposite markers as foll: k2, k2tog, yo, k3. Place a marker 5 (5¹/₂, 6, 6, 6¹/₂, 7)"/12.5 (14, 15, 15, 16.5, 18)cm down from shoulder on front and back. Set in sleeves between markers. Sew side and sleeve seams. Sew on buttons.

(See charts on page 134)

Bug Off

This little ladybug isn't quite ready to fly away home. Gitta Schrade's cropped tank, with adorable intarsia insect motif and striped edging, knits quickly in stockinette; striped drawstring shorts make a cool companion piece. "Bug Off" first appeared in the Spring/Summer '98 issue of *Family Circle Easy Knitting* magazine.

MATERIALS

Top
- ▣ *Saucy* by Reynolds, 3½oz/100g balls, each approx 185yd/169m (cotton) Top
  1 (1, 1, 2) balls in #341 coral (MC)
  1 ball each in #899 black (A), #365 pink (B), #358 red (C) and #130 sunburst (D)

Shorts
  1 ball each in #899 black (A), #365 pink (B), #358 red (C), #130 sunburst (D) and
  341 coral (MC)

Both
- ▣ One pair each sizes 5 and 7 (3.75 and 4.5 mm) needles OR SIZE TO OBTAIN GAUGE
- ▣ Sizes 5 and 7 (3.75 mm and 4.5mm) circular needle, 16"/40cm long
- ▣ Stitch holder
- ▣ Tapestry needle
- ▣ 8 beads (for shorts)

SIZES

Sized for Child's 2 (4, 6, 8). Shown in size 6.

FINISHED MEASUREMENTS

Top
- ▣ Chest 24 (26, 28, 30)"/61 (66, 71, 76)cm
- ▣ Length 7 (8, 9, 11)"/18 (20.5, 23, 28)cm

Shorts
- ▣ Hip 22 (24, 26, 28)"/56 (61, 66, 71)cm
- ▣ Length 6½ (7, 7½, 8½)"/16.5 (18, 19, 21.5)cm

GAUGE

20 sts and 28 rows to 4"/10 cm over St st using larger needles.
TAKE TIME TO CHECK YOUR GAUGE.

TOP

BACK

With smaller needles and MC, cast on 60 (65, 70, 75) sts. Work in St st for 4 rows. K1 row with A. **Next row (WS)** With A, knit (turning ridge). Change to larger needles. Cont in St st and stripes as foll: 2 rows B, 2 rows MC, 2 rows C, 2 rows B, then cont with MC until piece measures 3½ (3½, 4, 5½)"/9 (9.5, 10, 14)cm above turning ridge, end with a WS row.

Armhole shaping

Next row (RS) Bind off 4 sts at beg of next 2 rows, 3 sts at beg of next 2 rows, 2 sts at beg of next 4 rows, dec 1 st each side every other row 1 (1, 2, 3) times—36 (41, 44, 47) sts. Work even until piece measures 5 (5½, 6¼, 8)"/12.5 (14, 16, 20.5)cm above turning ridge.

Neck shaping

Next row (RS) Work 15 (16,17,17) sts, join 2nd ball and bind off center 6 (9, 10, 13) sts, work to end. Working both sides at once, bind off from neck edge 3 sts once, 2 sts once, then dec 1 st every other row twice—8 (9,10, 10) sts. Work even until piece measures 7 (8, 9, 11)"/18 (20.5, 23, 28)cm above turning ridge, end with a WS row. Bind off.

FRONT

Work as for back until piece measures 4½ (5, 5¾, 7½)"/11.5 (12.5, 14.5, 19)cm above turning ridge, end with a WS row. Shape neck and complete as for back.

FINISHING

Block pieces to measurements. Duplicate stitch ladybug, chart 2 (see page 137), to center front. Sew shoulder seams.

Armhole band

With RS facing, larger needles and C, pick up and k 50 (54, 58, 60) sts along each armhole edge as foll: 1 row C; change to smaller needles; 2 rows B. Bind off with D.

Neckband

With RS facing, larger circular needle and C, pick up and k 84 (90, 100, 108) sts around neck edge. **Rnd 1 (WS)** With C, purl. Change to smaller needles. **Rnd 2** With B, knit. **Rnd 3** With B, purl. Bind off with D. Sew side seams. Fold lower edge hem to WS at turning ridge and sew in place.

SHORTS

Stripe pat

*2 rows B, 2 rows MC, 2 rows C, 2 rows A, 2 rows D, 4 rows MC, 2 rows B, 2 rows C, 2 rows A, 4 rows B, 2 rows MC, 2 rows A; rep from * for stripe pat.

LEG

With smaller needles and MC, cast on 66 (71, 76, 81) sts. Work in St st for 4 rows. K 1 row with A. **Next row (WS)** With A, knit (turning ridge). Change to larger needles. Cont in St st and

(Continued on page 135)

Beach Patrol

for intermediate knitters

As light as the ocean breeze, Jacqueline Van Dillen's lacy V-neck pullover is ideal for seaside escapes. Highlighted with duplicate stitch floral accents and delicate eyelets, it's knitted in coolest cotton. "Beach Patrol" first appeared in the Spring/Summer '99 issue of *Family Circle Easy Knitting* magazine.

MATERIALS

- *Millefili Fine* by Filatura Di Crosa/Stacy Charles, 1³⁄₄oz/50g balls, each approx 136yd/125m (cotton)
  5 (6, 8, 9) balls in #69 white (MC)
- Embroidery Floss by DMC, 8.7yd/8m (cotton)
  1 skein each in #3609 pink (A), #472 green (B), #211 lilac (C) and #272 yellow (D)
- One pair size 5 (3.75mm) needles OR SIZE TO OBTAIN GAUGE
- Size 3 (3mm) circular needle, 16"/40cm long
- Tapestry needle

SIZES

Sized for Child's 4, 6, 8, 10. Shown in size 6.

FINISHED MEASUREMENTS

- Chest 28 (32, 37, 41¹⁄₂)"/71 (81, 94, 105.5)cm
- Length 15¹⁄₂ (17¹⁄₄, 19, 20³⁄₄)"/39.5 (43.5, 48, 53)cm
- Upper arm 12 (13, 14, 15)"/30.5 (33, 35.5, 38)cm

GAUGE

21 sts and 32 rows to 4"/10cm over chart 1 or 2 using size 5 (3.75mm) needles.
TAKE TIME TO CHECK YOUR GAUGE.

Notes

1 Be sure that there is always a yo to compensate for each dec in every row to keep the st count the same. If there is not, then omit the yo or dec and work st in St st.
2 Always work first and last st in St st for selvage sts.

BACK

With MC, cast on 75 (87, 99, 111) sts. K 2 rows.

Beg chart 1

Row 1 (RS) Work first 2 sts of chart, work 12-st rep 5 (6, 7, 8) times, work last 13 sts of chart. Cont in pat as established until 70 (80, 90, 100) rows of chart have been worked—piece measures approx 9 (10¹⁄₄, 11¹⁄₂, 12³⁄₄)"/23 (26, 29, 32.5)cm from beg.

Beg chart 2

Next row (RS) Work first 5 sts of chart, work 12-st rep 5 (6, 7, 8) times, work last 10 sts of chart. Cont in pat as established, for 1 row more.

Armhole shaping

Cont chart pat, bind off 3 (3, 4, 4) sts at beg of next 2 rows, 3 sts at beg of next 0 (0, 0, 2) rows, 2 sts at beg of next 0 (0, 4, 4) rows, dec 1 st each side every other row 3 (4, 3, 4) times—63 (73, 77, 81) sts. (**Note**: After 18 rows of chart 2 have been worked, cont to rep rows 3-18 for pat). Work even until armhole measures 6¹⁄₂ (7, 7¹⁄₂, 8)"/16.5 (17.5, 19, 20.5)cm. Bind off all sts.

FRONT

Work as for back until armhole measures 2¹⁄₂ (3, 3, 3¹⁄₂)"/6.5 (7, 7, 9)cm, end with a WS row.

Neck shaping

Next row (RS) Work 31 (36, 38, 40) sts, place center st on a holder, join 2nd ball and work to end. Working both sides at once, dec 1 st at each neck edge every other row 14 (15, 15, 16) times. Work even until same length as back. Bind off rem 17 (21, 23, 24) sts each side for shoulders.

SLEEVES

With MC, cast on 41 sts.

Beg chart 1

Row 1 (RS) K1, work first 2 sts of chart, work 12-st rep twice, work last 13 sts of chart, k1.

Cont in pat as established, inc 1 st each side (working inc sts into chart pat at 1 st in from edge) every 6th row 0 (10, 13, 20) times, every 8th row 12 (5, 4, 0) times—65 (71, 75, 81) sts. Work even until piece measures 13 (14, 15, 16)"/33 (35.5, 38, 40.5)cm from beg.

Cap shaping

Bind off 3 sts at beg of next 20 rows. Bind off rem 5 (11, 15, 21) sts.

FINISHING

Block pieces to measurements.

Embroidery

With A, B, C and D and tapestry needle, work duplicate st embroidery foll chart for placement and photo for colors.

Neckband

Sew shoulder seams. With RS facing, circular needle and MC, beg at back neck, pick up and k 93 (97, 97, 101) sts evenly around neck edge, including center front st on holder. Join and work in k1, p1 rib as foll: rib to 2 sts before center st, k2tog, k1, SKP, rib to end. Cont in this way to dec 1 st each side of center st every other rnd until band measures ³⁄₄"/2cm. Bind off loosely in rib. Set in sleeves. Sew side and sleeve seams.

(See charts on page 136)

Fringe Benefits

Brighten her day with this fiery pullover. Jean Schafer-Albers's swing top knits in a flash in simple stockinette; trim it with winsome fringe for a trendy topper. "Fringe Benefits" first appeared in the Spring/Summer '01 issue of *Family Circle Easy Knitting* magazine.

MATERIALS

- *Imagine* by Classic Elite Yarns, 1³⁄₄oz/50g balls, each approx 93yd/85m (cotton)
  3 (3, 4, 4) balls in #9230 pink
- One pair size 6 (4mm) needles OR SIZE TO OBTAIN GAUGE
- Size 6 (4mm) circular needle 16"/40cm long
- Size B/1 (2mm) crochet hook
- Stitch holders

SIZES

Sized for child's 2 (4, 6, 8). Shown in size 4.

FINISHED MEASUREMENTS

- Chest 25 (26¹⁄₂, 28, 29¹⁄₂)"/63.5 (67, 71, 75)cm
- Length 11¹⁄₂ (13, 14, 16¹⁄₂)"/29 (33, 35.5, 42)cm
- Upper arm 9 (9¹⁄₂, 10¹⁄₂, 11¹⁄₂)"/23 (24, 26.5, 29)cm

GAUGE

21 sts and 27 rows to 4"/10cm over St st using larger needles.
TAKE TIME TO CHECK YOUR GAUGE.

BACK

With larger needles, cast on 2 sts. Working in St st, work 1 row even. Cast on 2 sts at beg of next 2 (4, 0, 4) rows, 3 sts at beg of next 20 (20, 24, 24) rows—66 (70, 74, 82) sts. Work even until piece measures 6¹⁄₂ (7¹⁄₂, 8, 10)"/16.5 (19, 20.5, 25.5)cm. from beg, end with a WS row.

Armhole shaping

Bind off 2 (3, 3, 3) sts at beg of next 4 (2, 2, 2) rows, 0 (2, 2, 2) sts at beg of next 2 rows, dec 1 st each side every other row 2 (3, 1, 4) times—54 (54, 62, 64) sts. Work even until armhole measures 5 (5¹⁄₂, 6, 6¹⁄₂)"/12.5 (14, 15, 16.5)cm.

Neck shaping

K14 (14, 16, 17) sts and place on holder, bind off center 26 (26, 30, 30) sts for back neck, k14 (14, 16, 17) sts and place on holder.

FRONT

Work as for back until armhole measures 2³⁄₄ (3¹⁄₄, 3¹⁄₂, 4¹⁄₄)"/7 (8, 9, 10.5)cm.

Neck shaping

Next row (RS) Work 22 (22, 26, 27) sts, join 2nd ball of yarn and bind off center 10 sts, work to end. Working both sides at once, cont to bind off from neck edge 3 sts 1 (1, 2, 2) times, 2 (2, 0, 0) sts 1 (1, 0, 0) time, dec 1 st each side every other row 3 (3, 4, 4) times—14 (14, 16, 17) sts rem each side. When same length as back, place sts on holder for each shoulder.

SLEEVES

Cast on 44 (46, 50, 52) sts. P 1 row on WS, then cont in St st, inc 1 st each side on next row, then every other row 1 (1, 2, 3) times more—48 (50, 56, 60) sts. Work even until piece measures ¹⁄₄ (³⁄₄, 1¹⁄₄, 1)"/.5 (2, 3, 2.5)cm from beg, end with a WS row.

Cap shaping

Bind off 2 (3, 3, 3) sts at beg of next 4 (2, 2, 2) rows, 2 sts at beg of next 0 (2, 2, 2) rows, dec 1 st each side of next row, then every other row 4 (9, 10, 12) times. Bind off 2 sts at beg of next 10 (4, 4, 4) rows. Bind off rem 10 (10, 16, 16) sts.

FINISHING

Block pieces to measurements. Join shoulders using 3-needle bind-off as follows: with the right side of the 2 pieces facing each other and the needles parallel, insert a third needle knitwise into the first st of each needle, k these 2 sts tog and slip them off the needle. *K the next 2 sts tog in the same way. Slip the first st on the 3rd needle over the 2nd st and off the needle; rep from * until all sts are bound off.

Neckband

With RS facing and circular needle, pick up and k 82 (82, 86, 90) sts evenly around neck edge. Join and work in k1, p1 rib for 6 rnds. Bind off loosely in rib.

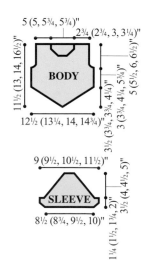

Light and Lacy

for intermediate knitters

Let her soak up the sun with a smile. Jacqueline Jewitt's airy vest charms with a diamond and eyelet pattern and sweet embroidered daisies. "Light and Lacy" first appeared in the Spring/Summer '99 issue of *Family Circle Easy Knitting* magazine.

MATERIALS

- *J&P Coats* Speed Cro-Sheen*® by Coats & Clark, 100yd/91m balls (cotton)
  5 (6) balls in #1 white
- J&P Coats® Embroidery Floss 8.7yd/8m skeins (cotton)
  4 skeins in #212 lilac and #201 pink
  6 skeins in #214 green
- Size 3 (3mm) circular needle OR SIZE TO OBTAIN GAUGE
- One pair size 3 (3mm) needles
- Size 1 (2mm) steel crochet hook
- Five ⅜"/15mm buttons

SIZES
Sized for girl's 4 (6). Shown in size 4.

FINISHED MEASUREMENTS
- Chest 29½ (33¼)"/75 (84.5)cm
- Length 13½ (14¼)"/34 (37.5)cm

GAUGE
22 sts and 34 rows to 4"/10cm over chart pat using size 3 (3mm) needles.
TAKE TIME TO CHECK YOUR GAUGE.

BODY
Beg at lower edge, with circular needle, cast on 163 (183) sts. K 4 rows.

Beg chart pat
Row 1 (RS) Work 20-st rep of chart 8 (9) times, end with st 23. Cont to foll chart pat, rep rows 1-20 three times and piece measures approx 7¼"/18.5cm from beg. Separate for fronts and back **Next row (RS)** Work 38 (44) sts for right front, bind off 8 sts for armhole, work 71 (79) sts for back, bind off 8 sts for armhole, work 38 (44) sts for left front. Leaving first 2 sets of sts for right front and back on circular needle, work the last 38 (44) sts for left front only with straight needles.

LEFT FRONT
Neck and armhole shaping
Next row (WS) Work even. **Next row (RS)** Dec 1 st at beg (armhole edge) and dec 1 st at end (neck edge) of row. Cont to dec 1 st at armhole edge every other row 3 (4) times and dec 1 st at neck edge every other row 12 (14) times more—21 (24) sts rem. Work even in pat until row 20 (10) of 5th (6th) 20-row rep is completed and armhole measures approx 4¾ (6)"/11 (15)cm. Bind off.

BACK
Rejoin yarn to 71 (79) sts of back and work 1 WS row even. Then dec 1 st at each armhole edge on next row and every other row 3 (4) times more—63 (69) sts. Work even until armhole measures 3¾ (5)"/9.5 (12.5)cm.

Neck shaping
Next row (RS) Work 24 (27) sts, join 2nd ball of yarn and bind off center 15 sts, work to end. Working both sides at once, dec 1 st at each neck edge every other row 3 times. When same number of rows as left front, bind off rem 21 (24) sts each side for shoulders.

RIGHT FRONT
Rejoin yarn and work to correspond to left front, reversing shaping.

FINISHING
Block pieces to measurements.

Embroidery
Work embroidery on fronts only. Using eyelet holes in center of St st diamonds as a center, embroider lazy daisy sts in alternating pinks and purples as in photo. Embroider leaves in green around flowers. Sew shoulder seams.

Armhole picot edging
With crochet hook, work sc evenly all around armhole. Join and ch 1. Rnd 2 * 1 sc in each of 3 sc, ch 3; rep from * around. Join and fasten off. With crochet hook, beg at lower left front corner, work an edge of sc in each st along lower edge, 37 sc along each center front and evenly along neck of vest. Join and fasten off.

Lower shell edge
With crochet hook, join with sl st in left front lower corner, work 1 (0) sc in st with joining, *ch 7, skip 1 sc, sc in next sc, ch 7, skip 5 sc, sc in next sc; rep from * 19 (22) times more, ending last rep ch 7, sk 1 (4) sc, sc in last sc—21 (23) ch-7 lps. Ch 1, turn. **Row 2** Sc in first sc, sl st into 4th ch of ch-7 for size 6 only, then *[ch 2, 1 dc] 7 times into ch-7 lp, 1 sl into 4th ch of next ch-7; rep from *, end [ch 2, 1 dc] 7 times into ch-7 lp, sl st in last sc. Ch 1, turn. **Row 3** Work 2 sc in each ch-2 sp and 1 sc in each sl st across, fasten off.

Picot edge
Rejoin yarn from RS at left front shoulder. Rnd 1 Sc in same st with joining, sc in each of next 2 sc, *ch 3, sc in each of next 3 sc; rep from * to beg of neck shaping, work 37 sc evenly along straight front edge, then cont picot edge along shell edge as foll: [sc in 3 sc, ch 3] 4 times, sc in

(Continued on page 136)

Norah Gaughan's sun-kissed halters with easy eyelets are perfect at poolside, but don't stop there. Shade the sun with Jacqueline Van Dillen's rolled brim hat and tote the essentials in Veronica Manno's candy-colored bags. "Shore Things" first appeared in the Spring/Summer '01 issue of *Family Circle Easy Knitting* magazine.

MATERIALS
Bag
- *Raffia* by Judi & Co., 72yd/66m hanks (rayon)
  2 balls in fuchsia or tomato
- Size J/10 (6mm) crochet hook OR SIZE TO OBTAIN GAUGE

Hat
- 2 balls in fuchsia
- Size G/6 (4.5mm) crochet hook OR SIZE TO OBTAIN GAUGE

Halter
- Tucson by Reynolds/JCA, 1³/₄oz/50g balls, each approx 118yd/108m (cotton/acrylic)
  2 balls in #56 pink or #24 apricot
- One pair each sizes 5 and 7 (3.75mm and 4.5mm) needles OR SIZE TO OBTAIN GAUGE
- Two size 7 (4.5mm) dpn for I-cord

SIZES
Hat
One size to fit child's 4 to 8.
Halter
Sized for child's 4 (6). Shown in both sizes.

FINISHED MEASUREMENTS
Bag
- Approx 9"/23cm wide by 8"/20.5cm long (without handles)

Hat
- Circumference: Approx 19"/48.5cm

Halter
- Chest 23 (26 1/2)"/58.5 (67.5)cm
- Length 11 (12)"/ 28 (30.5)cm

GAUGES
Bag
- 2 clusters and 4 rows to 4"/10cm over cluster pat using size J/10 (6mm) crochet hook.

Hat
- 17 sts and 8 rows to 4"/10cm over dc using size G/6 (4.5mm) crochet hook.

Halter
- 19 sts and 28 rows to 4"/10cm over St st using larger needles.

TAKE TIME TO CHECK YOUR GAUGE.

STITCHES USED
Cluster pattern (for bag)
Rnd 1 Ch 3, *skip 2 sts, in the next st work 2 tr, ch 1 and 2 tr, (cluster), skip 2 sts, 1 tr in next st; rep from * to last st, join with a sl st to top of ch-3.

Rnd 2 Ch 3, *work 1 cluster in next ch-1 sp of the previous cluster, 1 tr in the next tr; rep from * to last cluster, work cluster then join rnd with sl st to top of ch-3.

Rep rnd 2 for cluster pat.

Pattern stitch (for hat)
Rnd 1 *Skip 1 st, work 3 dc in next st, skip 1 st; rep from * around.

Rnd 2 *[Yo, insert hook in next dc, yo and draw through 2 lps] in each of next 3 sc, yo and draw through 4 lps on hook, ch 2; rep from * around.

BAG
Beg at bottom edge, ch 20.

Rnd 1 Work 3 dc into the 2nd ch from hook, dc in each ch to last ch, do not turn, work 3 dc in the last ch, working along the other side of ch, work 1 dc in the back of each ch. Join with sl st to top of first dc.

Rnd 2 Ch 1, 2 dc in the next 3 dc, dc in each dc to corner 3 dc, work 2 dc in each of these 3 dc, dc to end of rnd. Join with sl st to top of first dc.

Rnd 3 Ch 1, work dc around, work 2 dc over each corner 3 dc. Join.

Rnd 4 Rep rnd 3.

Rnds 5-10 Work in cluster pat (there are 10 clusters in rnd).

Rnd 11 Work sc in each st and ch-1 sp. Fasten off.

HANDLES (make 2)
Make a ch 16"/40.5cm long. Dc in the 2nd ch from hook and in each ch to last ch, do not turn, work 3 dc in the last dc, work 1 dc in each dc on the other side of ch. Join with sl st to top of first dc. Fasten off. Sl st each end of handle to top edge of bag.

HAT
Ch 5. Join with sl st to first ch to form ring.
Note
Ch 3 at beg of every rnd (this counts as first dc).

Rnd 1 Ch 3 (counts as 1 dc), work 15 dc in ring—16 dc.

Rnd 2 Ch 3, work 1 dc in same st, work 2 dc in each dc—32 dc.

Rnd 3 Ch 3, work dc in same st, *dc in next dc, work 2 dc in next; rep from * around—48 dc.

Rnd 4 Ch 3, *dc in next dc, 2 dc in next dc, dc in next dc; rep from * around—64 dc.

Rnd 5 Ch 3, [dc in next 12 dc, 2 dc in next dc] 4 times, dc in next 11 dc, 2 dc in next dc—69 dc.

Rnds 6 and 7 Rep rnds 1 and 2 of pat st.

Rnd 8 Ch 3, [dc in next st, 2 dc in next ch-2 sp] twice, [dc in next st, 3 dc in ch-2 sp, dc in next st, 2 dc in ch-2 sp] 10 times, dc in next st, 2 dc in last ch-2 sp—79 dc.

Rnd 9 Ch 3, [work 2 dc in next dc, 1 dc in next 9 dc] 7 times, 2 dc in next dc, 1 dc in each dc to end of rnd—87 dc.

Rnds 10 and 11 Work rnds 1 and 2 of pat st.

Rnd 12 Ch 3, 2 dc in next ch-2 sp, [dc in next dc, 2 dc in next ch-2 sp] 6 times, dc in next dc, 3 dc in next ch-2 sp, [dc in next dc, 2 dc in next ch-2 sp] 7 times, dc in next dc, 3 dc in next ch-2 sp, [dc in next dc, 2 dc in next ch-2 sp] 7 times, dc in next dc, 3 dc in next ch-2 sp, [dc in next dc, 2 dc in next ch-2 sp] 4 times, dc in next dc, 3 dc in last ch-3 sp—91 dc.

Rnd 13 Work dc, inc 3 sts evenly around—94 dc.

Rnd 14 Work dc, inc 14 sts evenly around—108 dc.

Rnd 15 Work dc, inc 8 sts evenly around—116 dc

Rnd 16 Work dc, inc 5 sts evenly around—121 dc.

Rnd 17 Work dc in each dc.
Fasten off.

HALTER

BACK

With smaller needles, cast on 54 (62) sts. Work in k1, p1 rib for 3 rows, inc 1 st on last row—55 (63) sts. Change to larger needles and work in St st until piece measures 7 (7½)"/17.5 (19)cm. Change to smaller needles and work 1 more row in St st. Then work in k1, p1 rib for 2 rows. Bind off in rib.

FRONT

Work as for back until piece measures 5¾ (6½)"/14.5 (16.5)cm from beg, end with a WS row. Work front detail foll chart for desired size—3 sts rem each side.

I-CORD

With dpn, cont on rem 3 sts as foll: **Next row (RS)** K3, do not turn. Slide sts back to beg of needle to work next row from RS. Rep this row until cord measures 12 (13)"/30.5 (33)cm, or desired length. Pass first 2 sts over 3rd st and weave in ends.

FINISHING

Block pieces to measurements. Sew side seams.

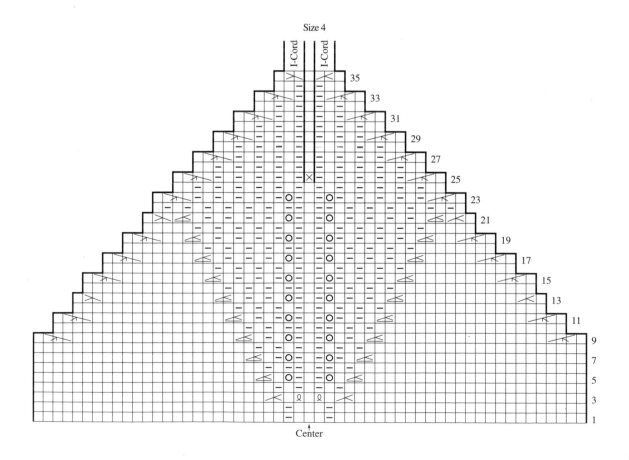

Size 4

Size 6

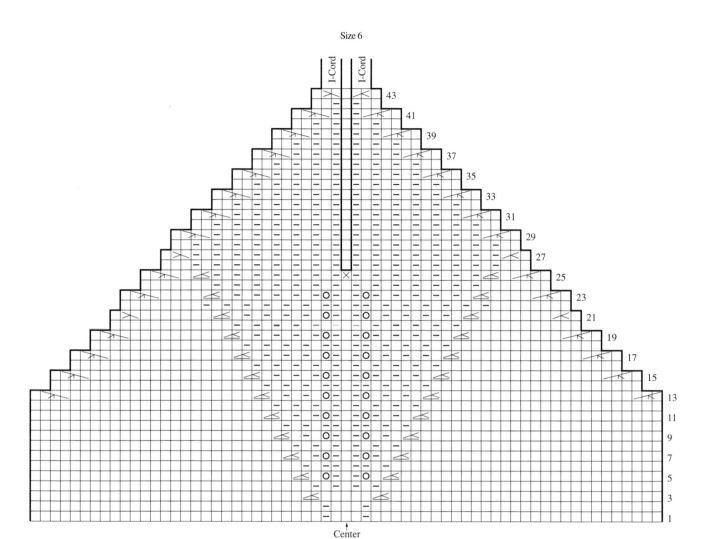

Stitch Key

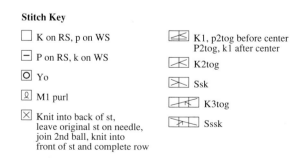

☐ K on RS, p on WS

− P on RS, k on WS

Ⓞ Yo

Ⓠ M1 purl

☒ Knit into back of st,
 leave original st on needle,
 join 2nd ball, knit into
 front of st and complete row

⬓ K1, p2tog before center
 P2tog, k1 after center

⬓ K2tog

⬓ Ssk

⬓ K3tog

⬓ Sssk

Warm-weather campouts require the right gear. His rugged pullover, designed by Anne E. Smith in traditional horseshoe cables with textured ringlet stitches, offers on-the-go comfort; Abigail Liles's textured patchwork cardigan is a sunny idea for cloudy days. "Trail Mix" first appeared in the Spring/Summer '98 issue of *Family Circle Easy Knitting* magazine.

MATERIALS

Girl's sweater

- *Provence* by Classic Elite, 4½oz/125g hanks, each approx 256yd/233m (cotton)
  1 (1, 2) hanks in #2601 white (A)
  1 hank each in #2633 yellow (B) and #2685 orange (C)
- One pair each sizes 5 and 6 (3.75 and 4mm) needles OR SIZE TO OBTAIN GAUGE
- Five ¾"/20mm buttons
- Bobbins
- Stitch markers

Boy's sweater

- *Figaro* by Unger, 1¾oz/50g skeins, each approx 104yd/96m (cotton/viscose/silk)
  7 (8, 9, 10) skeins in #14 blue
- One pair size 5 (3.75mm) needles OR SIZE TO OBTAIN GAUGE
- Size 4 (3.5mm) circular needle, 16"/40cm long
- Cable needle (cn)
- Stitch markers

GIRL'S

SIZES

Sized for Child's 2 (4, 6, 8). Shown in size 6.

FINISHED MEASUREMENTS

- Chest 25½ (29, 31)"/65 (73.5, 78.5)cm
- Length 11¼ (12¼, 13½)"/28.5 (31, 34.5)cm
- Upper arm 10 (11, 12)"/25 (28, 31)cm

GAUGE

22 sts and 32 rows to 4"/10cm over St st using larger needles.
TAKE TIME TO CHECK YOUR GAUGE.

Notes

1 Follow schematic drawing for placement of blocks.
2 When changing colors, twist yarns on WS to prevent holes. Use a separate bobbin of color for each block.
3 Work first row of a color change in St st to avoid p bump from showing on the RS.

STITCHES USED

Seed Stitch

Row 1 (RS) *K1, p1; rep from * to end. Row 2 K the purl sts and p the knit sts. Rep row 2 for seed st.

Block Pattern

Block A

With A, work in St st over 14 (16, 17) sts and 18 (20, 22) rows.

Block B

With B, work in seed st over 14 (16, 17) sts and 18 (20, 22) rows.

Block C

With C, work in reverse St st over 14 (16, 17) sts and 18 (20, 22) rows.

BACK

With smaller needles and A, cast on 70 (80, 85) sts. Work in seed st for 1"/2.5cm. Change to larger needles.

Beg color sequence

Next row (RS) Work blocks C, A, B, C, A. Cont as established foll schematic drawing for placement. Work last row of blocks over 10 (10, 12) rows. Bind off all sts.

LEFT FRONT

With smaller needles and A, cast on 33 (37, 40) sts. Work in seed st for 1"/2.5cm. Change to larger needles.

Beg color sequence

Next row (RS) Work blocks C, B, then 5 (5, 6) sts block A. Cont in pat as established, foll schematic drawing for placement, until piece measures 10 (11, 12)"/25.5 (28, 30.5)cm from beg, end with 1 row less than the last full set of color blocks.

Neck shaping

Next row (WS) Bind off 5 (5, 6) sts. work to end (neck edge). Cont to bind off from neck edge 2 sts twice, then dec 1 st every other row twice—22 (26, 28) sts. Work even until same length as back. Bind off.

RIGHT FRONT

Work to correspond to left front, foll schematic drawing for placement of blocks and reversing neck shaping.

LEFT SLEEVE

With smaller needles and A, cast on 36 (38, 41)

sts. Work in seed st for 1"/2.5cm. Change to larger needles.

Beg color sequence

Next row (RS) Work 11 (11, 12) sts B, 14 (16, 17) sts C, 11 (11, 12) sts A. Follow schematic drawing for block placement, AT SAME TIME, inc 1 st each side every 6th row 8 (8, 12) times, then every 8th row 2 (3, 1) times—56 (60, 67) sts. Work even until piece measures 9 (10, 11)"/23 (25.5, 28)cm from beg, end with an entire block pat. Bind off all sts.

RIGHT SLEEVE

Work as for left sleeve, foll color placement for right sleeve.

FINISHING

Block pieces to measurements. Sew shoulder seams.

COLLAR

With RS facing, smaller needles and A, beg at right front neck edge, pick up and k 51 (55, 57) sts evenly around neck edge. Work in seed st for 2½"/6.5cm. Bind off.

Button band

With smaller needles and A, pick up and k 55 (59, 65) sts evenly along left front. Work in seed st for 1"/2.5cm. Bind off. Place markers on band for 5 buttons, the first one 1"/2.5cm from upper edge, the last one ½"/1.25cm from lower edge and 3 others spaced evenly between.

Buttonhole band

Work as for button band, working buttonholes opposite markers on the 3rd row by yo, k2tog. Cont until band measures 1"/2.5cm. Bind off. Place markers 5 (5½, 6)"/12.5 (14, 15.5)cm down from shoulders on front and back. Sew top of sleeves between markers. Sew sleeve

and side seams. Sew on buttons.

BOY'S SWEATER

SIZES

Sized for Child's 2 (4, 6, 8). Shown in size 6.

FINISHED MEASUREMENTS

■ Chest 29 (32, 34½, 37)"/74 (81, 88, 94)cm
■ Length 15½ (16½, 17, 18)"/39.5 (40.5, 43, 45.5)cm
■ Upper arm 11 (12, 13, 14)"/28 (30, 33, 35)cm

GAUGES

■ 14 sts to 2"/5cm and 22 rows to 3"/7.5cm over cable pat using size 5 (3.75mm) needles.
■ 24 sts to 4"/10cm over ringlet st using size 5 (3.75mm) needles.
TAKE TIME TO CHECK YOUR GAUGES.

STITCHES USED

Ringlet Stitch

(over an even number of sts) **Row 1 (WS)** Purl. **Row 2** *Make ringlet (MR) as foll: p2, keeping yarn at front, sl these 2 st back to LH needle, bring yarn to back, passing in front of the 2 sts, sl sts back to RH needle; rep from *.
Rep rows 1 and 2 for ringlet st.

Cable Pattern (over 14 sts) **Row 1 (RS)** P1, sl next 3 sts to en and hold to back, k3, k3 from cn, sl next 3 sts to cn and hold to front, k3, k3 from cn, p1 **Rows 2-10** K the knit sts and p the purl sts. Rep rows 1-10 for cable pat.

BACK

With size 5 (3.75mm) needles, cast on 100 (108, 116, 124) sts.

Beg rib and ringlet st

Next row (WS) P3 (7, 11, 15), *[k2, p2] 3 times, k2, p6; rep from *, end last rep p3 (7, 11, 15). **Next row** K1, work row 2 of ringlet st over next 2 (6, 10, 14) sts, *[p2, k2] 3 times, p2, work row 2

of ringlet st over next 6 sts; rep from *, end last rep work row 2 of ringlet st over 2 (6, 10, 14) sts, k1. Cont in pat as established for 7 rows more.

Beg cable and ringlet st

Next row (RS) K1, cont ringlet st over next 2 (6, 10, 14) sts, *work cable pat over next 14 sts, cont ringlet st over next 6 sts; rep from *, end last rep cont ringlet st over 2 (6, 10, 14) sts, k1. Cont in pat as established until piece 15½ (16½, 17, 18)"/39.5 (40.5, 43, 45.5)cm from beg. Bind off all sts knitwise.

FRONT

Work as for back until piece measures 13 (14, 14½, 15½)"/33 (34, 36.5, 39)cm from beg, end with a WS row.

Neck shaping

Next row (RS) Work 37 (41, 45, 48) sts, join 2nd ball of yarn and bind off center 26 (26, 26, 28) sts, work to end. Working both sides at once, bind off from each neck edge 3 sts twice, 2 sts once, 1 st once. Work even until same length as back. Bind off rem 28 (32, 36, 39) sts each side for shoulder.

SLEEVES

With size 5 (3.75mm) needles, cast on 42 (42, 56, 56) sts.

Beg rib and ringlet st

Next row (WS) For sizes 2 and 4 only: [P2, k2] twice, p6, [k2, p2] 3 times, k2, p6, [k2, p2] twice. For sizes 6 and 8 only: P1, [k2, p2] 3 times, k2, *p6, [k2, p2] 3 times, k2; rep from * once more, p1. **Next row** For sizes 2 and 4 only: [K2, p2] twice, work row 2 of ringlet st over next 6 sts, [p2, k2] 3 times, p2, work row 2 of ringlet st over next 6 sts, [p2, k2] twice. For sizes 6 and 8 only: K1, [k2, p2] 3 times, p2, *work row 2 of ringlet st over next 6 sts, [k2, p2] 3 times, p2;

rep from * once more, k1. Cont in pat as established for 7 rows more.

Beg cable and ringlet st

Next row (RS) For sizes 2 and 4 only: K1, work last 7 sts cable pat, work row 2 of ringlet st over next 6 sts, work 14 sts cable pat, work row 2 of ringlet st over next 6 sts, work first 7 sts cable pat, k 1. For sizes 6 and 8 only: K1, *work 14 sts cable pat, work ringlet st over next 6 sts; rep from * once more, work 14 sts cable pat, k1. Cont in pat as established, inc 1 st each side (for sizes 2 and 4: work first 7 incs into cable pat to have a full 14-st cable, then rem sts into ringlet st; for sizes 6 and 8: work all incs into ringlet st), every other row 7 (10, 0, 2) times, every 4th row 9 (10,16, 17) times—74 (82, 88, 94) sts. Work even until piece measures 9 (10½, 11, 12)"/23 (26.5, 28, 30.5)cm from beg. Bind off all sts knitwise.

FINISHING

Sew shoulder seams. Place markers 6 (6½, 7, 7½)"/15 (16.5, 17.5, 19)cm down from shoulder seams on fronts and back for armholes. Sew top of sleeve, stretching to fit, to front and back between markers. Sew side and sleeve seams.

Neckband

With RS facing and circular needle, pick up and k 100 (100, 100, 104) sts evenly around neck edge. Join and work in k2, p2 rib for 10 rnds. Using larger needle, bind off, working k2, p2tog while binding off.

GIRL'S SWEATER

BACK

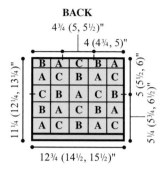

RIGHT FRONT   **LEFT FRONT**

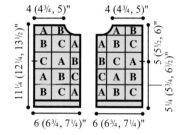

SLEEVES

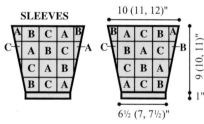

BOY'S SWEATER

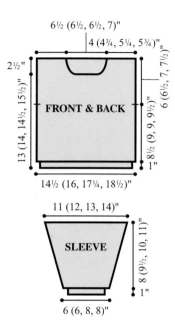

Tickled Pink

for intermediate knitters

Cool her down in a super sundress. Michelle Woodford's enchanting design is as easy to make as it is to wear. The eyelet button-front bodice is simply stitched to a gathered rectangle of cool cotton gingham. "Tickled Pink" first appeared in the Spring/Summer '98 issue of *Family Circle Easy Knitting* magazine.

MATERIALS
- *Cable 2005* by Sesia/Lane Borgosesia, 1¾oz/50g balls, each approx 146yd/135m (cotton)
  2 (2, 3) balls in #51 white
- One pair each sizes 3 and 4 (3 and 3.5mm) needles OR SIZE TO OBTAIN GAUGE.
- Four ⅜"/15mm buttons
- Stitch holders
- ¾yd/.7m of 45"/140cm wide fabric

SIZES
Sized for Child's 2 (4, 6). Shown in size 4.

FINISHED MEASUREMENTS
- Chest 22 (25, 27)"/56 (63.5, 68.5)cm
- Length 8¾ (8¾, 10)"/19.5 (22, 25.5)cm

GAUGE
24 sts and 32 rows to 4"/10cm over chart 2 using larger needles.
TAKE TIME TO CHECK YOUR GAUGE.

Note
When shaping, do not work partial eyelet pats, but work these sts in St st.

STITCHES USED
SK2P Sl 1, k2tog, psso
Left Front Band Pattern (over 6 sts)
Row 1 (RS) [P1, k1] twice, k 2nd st on LH needle working behind first st, k first st, drop both sts from LH needle (Left Twist-LT) **Row2** P2, [k1, p1] twice. Rep rows 1 and 2 for left front band pat.
Right Front Band Pattern (over 6 sts)
Row 1 (RS) K next 2 sts tog but do not drop from LH needle, k first st once more, drop both sts from LH needle (Right Twist—RT), [k1, p1] twice. **Row 2** [P1, k1] twice, p2. Rep rows 1 and 2 for right front band pat.

BACK
With larger needles, cast on 66 (74, 82) sts. Beg chart 1 Beg and end as indicated, and beg with a WS row, work 7 rows of chart 1. Work 2 (4, 8) rows in St st.

Beg chart 2
(see page 137)
Next row (RS) K0 (4, 8), work 13-st rep of chart 5 times, work first 0 (0, 9) sts once more, k1 (5, 0). Cont as established until piece measures 2¾ (3¼, 4)"/7 (8, 10)cm from beg, end with a WS row.

Armhole shaping
Bind off 4 sts at beg of next 0 (2, 2) rows, 2 sts at beg of next 4 (2, 2) rows. Dec 1 st each side on next row—56 (60, 68) sts. Work even until armhole measures 4 (4½, 5)"10 (11.5, 13)cm, end with a WS row.

Neck shaping
Next row (RS) Work 17 (19, 22) sts, join 2nd ball of yarn and bind off center 22 (22, 24) sts, work to end. Working both sides at once, bind off from each neck edge 3 sts once, 2 sts once, 1 st once. Work even until armhole measures 5 (5½, 6)"/12.5 (14, 15.5)cm. Bind off rem 11 (13, 16) sts each side for shoulders.

FRONT
Work as for back until 7 rows of chart #1 have been worked. Divide for fronts.
Next row (RS) K30 (34, 38) sts, work next 6 sts in left front border pat, place rem 30 (34, 38) sts on a holder for right front. Cont on left front sts only, and cont as for back, but working buttonholes in 6-st border, with the first one ½"/1.5cm above dividing row, the last one 3 rows below neck, and two others spaced evenly between, as foll: On a RS row, work to last 4 sts, yo, k2tog, work to end. When same length as back to armhole, shape armhole at side edge (beg of RS rows) as for back—31 (33, 37) sts. Work even until armhole measures 2½ (2½, 3)"/6.5 (6.5, 8)cm, end with a RS row.

Neck shaping
Next row (WS) Work 10 sts and place on a holder, work to end. Bind off from neck edge (beg of WS rows) 2 sts 4 times, then dec 1 st every other row 2 (2, 3) times—11 (13, 16) sts. Work even until same length as back. Bind off rem sts for shoulder.

Right front
Next row (RS) Pick up and k6 sts behind 6 border sts of left front, work sts from holder. Cont on 36 (40, 44) sts and work to correspond to left front, reversing shaping.

FINISHING
Block pieces to measurements. Sew shoulder seams.

Neckband
With RS facing and smaller needles, pick up

(Continued on page 137)

Ladybug, Ladybug

for intermediate knitters

A row of spunky spotted critters parades across the hem of Gitta Schrade's stripe-trimmed V-neck pullover. (Instructions for the complementing drawstring shorts appear on page 68.) "Ladybug, Ladybug" first appeared in the Spring/Summer '98 issue of *Family Circle Easy Knitting* magazine.

MATERIALS

- Saucy by Reynolds, 3½oz/100g balls, each approx 185yd/169m (cotton)
  2 (3, 3, 4) balls in #130 sunburst (MC)
  1 ball each in #341 coral (A), #358 red (B), #365 pink (C) and #899 black (D)
- One pair each sizes 5 and 7 (3.75 and 4.5mm) needles OR SIZE TO OBTAIN GAUGE
- Sizes 5 and 7 (3.75 mm and 4.5mm) circular needle, 16"/40cm long
- Stitch holder
- Tapestry needle
- 8 beads (for shorts)

SIZES

Sized for Child's 2 (4, 6, 8). Shown in size 6.

FINISHED MEASUREMENTS

- Chest 27½ (30, 32½, 35)"/70 (76, 82.5, 89)cm
- Length 15 (17, 19, 20)"/38 (43, 48, 51)cm
- Upper arm 13 (14, 15, 16)733 (36, 38, 40)cm

GAUGE

20 sts and 28 rows to 4710 cm over Chart 1 using larger needles.
TAKE TIME TO CHECK YOUR GAUGE.

Note

Ladybugs are embroidered with Duplicate st after pieces are knit.

BACK

With smaller needles and A, cast on 69 (75, 81, 87) sts. Work in St st for 5 rows, end with a RS row. **Next row (WS)** Knit (turning ridge). Change to larger needles. Cont in St st and stripes as foll: 2 rows A, 2 rows B, 2 rows C, 2 rows A, 2 rows B, 2 rows C, 2 rows MC, 2 rows A, 20 rows MC. Cont with MC to end of piece as foll: Beg and end as indicated, work foll chart 1 until piece measures 14 (16, 18, 19)"/35.5 (40.5, 45.5, 48.5)cm above turning ridge, end with a WS row.

Neck shaping

Next Row (RS) Work 28 (30, 32, 34) sts, join 2nd ball and bind off center 13(15, 17, 19) sts, work to end. Working both sides at once, bind off from each neck edge 3 sts twice. Bind off rem 22 (24, 26, 28) sts each side for shoulders.

FRONT

Work as for back until piece measures 10 (11½, 13¼, 13½)"/25.5 (29, 33.5, 34.5)cm above turning ridge, end with a WS row.

V-neck shaping

Next Row (RS) Work 34 (37, 40, 43) sts, place center st on a holder, join 2nd ball of yarn and work to end. Working both sides at once, dec 1 st at each each neck edge every other row 9 (10, 11, 10) times, every 4th row 3 (3, 3, 5) times—22 (24, 26, 28) sts. Work even until same length as back. Bind off rem sts each side for shoulders.

SLEEVES

With smaller needles and A, cast on 37 (39, 41, 43) sts. Work in St st for 5 rows, end with a RS row. Next row (WS) Knit (turning ridge). Change to larger needles. Cont in St st and stripes as for back then work in chart pat, AT SAME TIME, inc 1 st each side every 4th row 14 (15, 17, 18) times—65 (69, 75, 79) sts. Work even until piece measures 9 (10, 11, 12)"/23 (25.5, 28, 30.5)cm above turning ridge. Bind off.

FINISHING

Block pieces to measurements. Duplicate stitch ladybugs foll chart 2 on back and front. Sew shoulder seams.

Neckband

With RS facing, larger circular needle and MC, pick up and k 38 (41, 44, 49) sts along left front neck, k center st from holder (mark this st), pick up and k38 (41, 44, 49) sts along right front neck and 25 (27, 29, 31) sts along back neck—102 (110, 118, 130) sts. Join and work in St st in foll stripes: 2 rnds A, 2 rnds B, 2 rnds C, 2 rnds A, 1 rnd MC, AT SAME TIME, shape V every rnd: work to 1 st before center st, sl 2 sts tog knitwise, k1, psso. Change to smaller circular needle, and MC, p 1 rnd (turning ridge). Cont in MC until 2nd half of band measures same as first half, AT SAME TIME inc 1 st each side of center st every rnd. Bind off. Place markers 6½ (7, 7½, 8)"/16.5 (18, 19, 20)cm down from shoulders on front and back for armhole. Sew sleeves between markers. Sew side and sleeve seams. Fold hems to WS at turning ridge and sew in place.

(See schematics on page 137)

Awesome Accessories

Transform ordinary designs into different and dynamic works of art!

Hippie Chic
for beginner knitters

She'll adore this fashion flashback. Joanne Yardanou's hooded poncho is a cinch to make—simply knit two triangles, then stitch together and trim with chunky tassels. "Hippie Chic" first appeared in the Fall '00 issue of *Family Circle Easy Knitting* magazine.

MATERIALS
- *Imagine* by Lion Brand Yarn Co., 2½oz/70g balls, each approx 222yd/204m (acrylic/mohair)
  7 balls in #102 aqua
- Size 15 (10mm) circular needle, 36"/72cm long OR SIZE TO OBTAIN GAUGE
- Cable needle
- Size K/10½ (7mm) crochet hook

SIZES
One size fits all.

FINISHED MEASUREMENTS
- Lower edge 88"/223cm
- Length to neck 24"/61cm

GAUGE
10 sts and 13 rows to 4"/10cm over St st and 2 strands of yarn held tog using size 15 (10mm) needles.
TAKE TIME TO CHECK YOUR GAUGE.

RIGHT HALF
With 2 strands of yarn, cast on 110 sts. **Row 1 (RS)** K2, sl 2 sts to cn and hold to back, k1, k2tog from cn, k to last 5 sts, sl 1 st to cn and hold to front, k2tog, k1 from cn, k2. **Row 2** Purl. Rep these 2 rows 38 times more—32 sts.

Neck shaping
Next row (RS) Bind off 16 sts (front neck), k to last 5 sts, sl 1 st to cn and hold to front, k2tog, k1 from cn, k2 (back neck). P 1 row. **Next row** Dec 1 st, k to last 5 sts, work dec as before. Bind off rem 13 sts.

LEFT HALF
Work as for right half to neck shaping, end with a RS row.

Neck shaping
Next row (WS) Bind off 16 sts (front neck), p to end. **Next row** Work dec as before, k to last 2 sts, dec 1 st at end. P 1 row. Bind off rem 13 sts.

FINISHING
Block pieces lightly to measurements taking care not to flatten fabric. Sew center back seam, leaving front seam open.

HOOD
With circular needle and 2 strands of yarn, pick up and k 55 sts around neck edge. Work in St st for 12"/30.5cm. Bind off. Fold bound-off edge in half and sew tog for top of hood. With circular needle and 2 strands of yarn, pick up and k 54 sts around hood opening for facing. Working back and forth in rows, p 1 row, k 1 row, p 1 row. Bind off. Fold facing to inside and sew in place. Sew front seam. With crochet hook and 2 strands of yarn, work an edge of sc along lower edge of poncho.

Tassels (make 21)
Wind yarn 20 times around a 4½"/11cm piece of cardboard. Pull a strand through top of cardboard and cut lengths at opposite end. Draw one strand tightly around strands at 1"/2.5cm from top. Sew one tassel to top of hood. Sew other tassels evenly along lower edge of poncho.

TASSELS
Cut a piece of card board to the desired length of the tassel. Wrap yarn around the cardboard. Knot a piece of yarn tightly around one end, cut as shown, and remove the cardboard. Wrap and tie yarn around the tassel about 1"/2.5cm down from the top to secure the fringe.

Panda Pals

for intermediate knitters

Who wouldn't love these cuddly cuties? Linda Cyr's felted panda backpack and purse are sure to delight kids of all ages. Both accessories feature decorative pompom embellishments and I-cord finishing. "Panda Pals" first appeared in the Winter '96/'97 issue of *Family Circle Knitting* magazine.

MATERIALS

- *Nature Spun* by Brown Sheep 3½oz/100g skeins, each approx 245yd/224m
  3 skeins #N46 red (MC) 1 skein each #N89 brown (A), #N12 tan (B)
- One pair size 7 (4.5mm) needles OR SIZE TO OBTAIN GAUGE
- 1 set (4) dpn size 7 (4.5mm)
- Toggle button for backpack
- Yarn needle

FINISHED MEASUREMENTS

- Backpack about 8" x 11" x 4"/20 x 28 x 10cm
- Purse 6" x 6"/15 x 15cm

GAUGE

20 sts and 28 rows to 4"/10cm in St st before fulling.
TAKE TIME TO CHECK GAUGE.

STITCHES USED

Double Moss Stitch

Row 1(RS) *K2, p2; rep from *. **Rows 2 and 4 (WS)** K the knit sts and p the purl sts. **Row 3 (RS)** * P2, k2; rep from *. Rep rows 1-4 for double moss st pat.

I-Cord

With double pointed needles and A, cast on 4 sts. * K 1 row, do not turn but slide sts to other end of needle; rep from * to desired length. Bind off.

Note

Follow chart on page 36 to knit teddy bear motif. Embroider face after knit piece is felted.

BACKPACK

Bottom

With A, cast on 28 sts. Work 2 rows in Double Moss st. Cont in pat, inc 1 st at beg of each of next 12 rows—40sts. Work even until piece measures 4½"/11cm, end with a WS row. **Next row (RS)** Dec 1 st at beg of each of next 12 rows—28sts. Bind off.

Body

With MC, cast on 130 sts. Work in St st for 11"/28cm. Bind off.

Top flap

With MC, cast on 18 sts. Work 2 rows in double moss st. Cont in pat, inc 1 st at beg of each of next 12 rows—30sts. Work even until piece measures 7"/18cm, end with a WS row. Bind off.

Drawstring band

With MC, cast on 10 sts. Work in St st for 2½"/6.5cm, end with a WS row. * **Next row (RS)** K3, bind off 4 sts, k to end. **Next row (WS)** P3, cast on 4 sts, p3. Work even for 2¼"/5.5cm.* Rep from * to * 9 times more. Work in St st for 2½"/6cm—10 buttonholes made. Bind off.

Pocket

With MC, cast on 33 sts. Working in St st, work Bear chart to top of chart. Cont in MC only until piece measures 5¼"/13cm, end with WS row. Work in garter st for 1"/2.5cm. Bind off.

Strap

With A, cast on 10 sts. Work in St st for 40"/101.5cm. Bind off.

FINISHING

Sew cast on edge to bound off edge. Sew on bottom. Sew narrow ends of drawstring band tog, then sew to top. Sew cast-on edge of flap to back of pack along drawstring band seam. Sew pocket to front. Wash pack and strap in hot wash/cold rinse machine cycle. For added shrinkage, place pieces in dryer. Knit one length of I-cord to fit edge of flap plus 3"/7.5cm. Sew cord to edge of flap, looping cord at center for buttonloop. Knit another piece of I-cord 36"/91.5cm long. Lace cord through buttonholes of drawstring band. Tie knot at each end of cord, and tie cord ends in bow. Fold strap length in half and tack tog 3"/7.5cm from folded end for loop. Sew loop to center back of flap; sew ends of strap to back edge of bottom about 5"/12.5cm apart. Embroider bear face on pocket foll photo. Sew toggle button above pocket.

PURSE

With MC, cast on 33 sts. Work in garter st for 1"/2.5cm. Cont in St st for 4¼"/11cm, end with RS row. K 1 row for fold ridge. Working in St st, work Bear chart to top of chart. With MC only cont in St st until piece measures 10½"/26.5cm from beg. **Next row (RS)** Work in garter st, dec 1 st each side every other row row 10 times—3 sts. Sl 1, k2 tog, psso. Pull yarn through rem sts.

FINISHING

Fold piece at ridge. Sew sides. Wash in hot wash/cold rinse machine cycle. For added shrinkage, place pieces in dryer. Block purse to measurements until dry. Embroider bear face

(Continued on page 138)

Early Bloomer
for intermediate knitters

For heads-up on standout style, try Norah Gaughan's spiral stitched cap featuring reverse stockinette bands and embroidered flower trim. This topper is ahead of the curve. "Early Bloomer" first appeared in the Fall '00 issue of *Family Circle Easy Knitting* magazine.

MATERIALS
- *Eternity* by Reynolds/JCA, 1¾oz/50g balls, each approx 88yd/81m (wool/microfiber)
  1 ball in #778 dk pink (MC)
- *Paternayan Variegated Persian Yarn*, 8yd/7.4m skeins (wool)
  1 skein each in #14 gold multi (A) and #16 blue multi (B)
- One pair size 8 (5mm) needles OR SIZE TO OBTAIN GAUGE
- Tapestry needle for embroidery

SIZES
One size fits all.

FINISHED MEASUREMENTS
- 19"/48cm circumference

GAUGE
17 sts and 22 rows to 4"/10cm over St st using size 8 (5mm) needles.
TAKE TIME TO CHECK YOUR GAUGE.

HAT
With MC, cast on 82 sts. Work in St st for 2 rows.
Beg spiral pat
Row 1 (RS) K1, work 20-st rep of chart 4 times, k1. Cont to foll chart in this way through row 28. **Row 29** K1, p2tog, [k8, k2tog, p8, p2tog] 3 times, k8, k2tog, p8, k1. **Row 30** P1, [k9, p9] 4 times, p1. **Row 31** K9, [p9, k9] 3 times, p9, k2. **Row 32** P3, [k9, p9] 3 times, k9, p8. **Row 33** K5, k2tog, [p7, p2tog, k7, k2tog] 3 times, p7, p2tog, k4. **Row 34** P5, [k8, p8] 3 times, k8, p5. **Row 35** K2, k2tog, [p6, p2tog, k6, k2tog] 3 times, p6, p2tog, k6. **Row 36** P7, [k7, p7] 3 times, k7, p2. **Row 37** K1, [p5, p2tog, k5, k2tog] 4 times, k1. **Row 38** P1, k1, [p6, k6] 3 times, p6, k5, p1. **Row 39** K1, p2, p2tog, [k4, k2tog, p4, p2tog] 3 times, k4, k2tog, p2, k1. **Row 40** P1, k3, [p5, k5] 3 times, p5, k2, p1. **Row 41** K1, p1, [k3, k2tog, p3, p2tog] 3 times, k3, k2tog, p2, p2tog, k1. **Row 42** P1, [k4, p4] 4 times, p1. **Row 43** K2, k2tog, [p2, p2tog, k2, k2tog] 3 times, p2, p2tog, k2. **Row 44** P3, [k3, p3] 3 times, k3, p2. **Row 45** K1, [p1,

p2tog, k1, k2tog] 4 times, k1. **Row 46** P1, k1, [p2, k2] 3 times, p2, k1, p1. **Row 47** K1, [k2tog, k2] 4 times, k1. **Row 48** P14. **Row 49** [K2, k2tog] 3 times, k2. **Row 50** P11. Row 51 [K2, k2tog] twice, k3. **Row 52** P9. **Row 53** [K2, k2tog] twice, k1. **Row 54** P7. **Row 55** K1, [k2tog] 3 times. Pull yarn through rem 4 sts and draw up tightly to secure. Sew back seam.

FINISHING
Foll photo, embroider 4 alternating flowers in 12 petal lazy daisy st with contrast French knot centers.

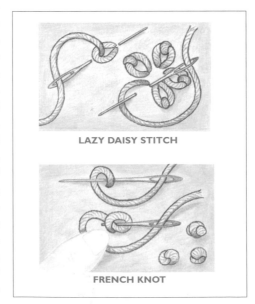

LAZY DAISY STITCH

FRENCH KNOT

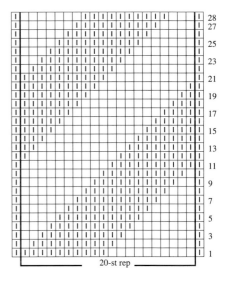

20-st rep

Stitch Key
- ⊞ K on RS, p on WS
- ☐ P on RS, k on WS

Stay one step ahead of the trends with this easy ensemble. Joanne Yordanou's cabled cape, hat and shoulder bag is the Gen-X alternative to the three-piece suit. "Teen Seen" first appeared in the Fall '00 issue of *Family Circle Easy Knitting* magazine.

MATERIALS

- *14-Ply* by Woolpak Yarns NZ/Baabajoes Wool Co., 8oz/250g hanks, each approx 310yd/286m (wool)
  4 hanks in lavender
- Size 10 (6mm) circular needle, 36"/92cm long OR SIZE TO OBTAIN GAUGE
- One set (5) size 10 (6mm) dpn
- One pair size 10 (6mm) needles
- Size G/6 (4.5mm) crochet hook
- Cable needle
- Stitch markers
- One ½"/13mm button

SIZES

Shown in one size.

FINISHED MEASUREMENTS

Cape
- Width at lower edge 52"/132cm
- Length 18"/45.5cm

Bag
- 13" x 10"/33cm x 25.5cm

Hat
- 21"/53cm circumference

GAUGE

16 sts and 20 rows/rnds to 4"/10cm over St st using size 10 (6mm) needles.
TAKE TIME TO CHECK YOUR GAUGE.

STITCH GLOSSARY

2-st LT
Skip first st and k into back of 2nd st on needle, then k first st and sl both sts from needle.

4-st RC
Sl 2 sts to cn and hold to back, k2, k2 from cn.

4-st LC
Sl 2 sts to cn and hold to front, k2, k2 from cn.

CABLE PANEL—in rnds
(over 16 sts)
Rnd 1 P1, 2-st LT, p1, k8, p1, 2-st LT, p1.
Rnds 2 and 4 P1, k2, p1, k8, p1, k2, p1.
Rnd 3 P1, 2-st LT, p1, 4-st LC, 4-st RC, p1, 2-st LT, p1.
Rep rnds 1-4 for cable panel.

To work in rows for bag:
Rows 2 and 4 K the knit and p the purl sts.

CAPE

Beg at neck edge with dpn, cast on 64 sts. Divide sts evenly on 4 needles. Join, taking care not to twist sts on needle. Mark end of rnd and sl marker every rnd. **Next rnd** *K2, p2; rep from * around. Cont in k2, p2 rib as established for 4"/10cm. **Note** Change to circular needle when there are too many sts to fit on dpn after increasing. Cont in pats as foll: **Rnd 1** K3, pm, k1, pm, k15, pm, k1, pm, k15, pm, k1, pm, work 16 sts in cable panel, pm, k1, pm, k11. **Rnd 2** *K to marked st, M1, k1, M1; rep from * twice more, work rnd 2 of cable panel, M1, k1, M1, k to end—8 sts inc'd. **Rnd 3** Work even as established. Cont to work in this way, maintaining 16 sts in cable panel, working 8 incs every other rnd by M1 each side of 4 marked sts 17 times more—208 sts. Work even (without incs) until cape measures 14½"/37cm from neck ribbing. **Next rnd** *K1, p1; rep from * around. **Next rnd** *P1, k1; rep from * around. Rep last 2 rnds for seed st until cape measures 15½"/39.5cm from neck ribbing. Bind off.

FINISHING

Block to measurements. Fold neckband in half to WS and sew in place.

HAT

Note

Hat is worked back and forth on straight needles.

First earflap

Cast on 7 sts. **Row 1 (WS)** Purl. Row 2 Inc 1 st, k to last st, inc 1 st. Rep last 2 rows 3 times more—15 sts. Cut yarn. Leave these sts on spare needle.

Second earflap

Work as for first earflap until there are 15 sts. Cast on 9 sts at beg of next WS row—24 sts, turn. P24, turn. Cast on 32 sts, k15 sts of first earflap, turn. Cast on 9 sts, p all 80 sts. **Next row (RS)** K38, p1, 2-st LT, p1, k38. **Next row** P38, k1, p2, k1, p38. Rep last 2 rows until piece measures 4"/10cm from last cast-on edge.

Top shaping

Row 1 (RS) K1, k2tog, k14, k2tog, k1, k2tog, k14, k2tog, p1, 2-st LT, p1, k2tog, k14, k2tog, k1, k2tog, k14, k2tog, k1—72 sts. **Row 2** P34, k1, p2, k1, p34. **Row 3** K1, k2tog, k12, k2tog, k1, k2tog, k12, k2tog, p1, 2-st LT, p1, k2tog, k12, k2tog, k1, k2tog, k12, k2tog, k1—64 sts. **Row 4** P30, k1, p2, k1, p30. Cont to dec 8 sts in this way every other row, having 2 sts less between decs twice more for 48 sts. Then dec in same way every 4th row 4 times—16 sts. **Next row (RS)** K1, k2tog, k1, k3tog, 2-st LT, k3tog, k1, k2tog,

(Continued on page 138)

Wrap Stars

You may not choose to wear Peggy McKenzie's colorful scarves all at once, but they stitch up so fast you make all four in no time. Each requires just one to two skeins of hand-dyed yarn; stitch up a bunch for the whole crowd. "Wrap Stars" first appeared in the Winter '99/'00 issue of *Family Circle Easy Knitting* magazine.

MATERIALS

Light blue scarf
- *Fandango* by Colinette/Unique Kolours, Ltd., 3¹⁄₂oz/100g hanks, each approx 108yd/100m (cotton): 1 hank in pale blue (A)
- *Mohair*, 3¹⁄₂oz/100g hanks, each approx 190yd/175m (mohair/wool/nylon): 1 hank in #101 Monet (B)
- One pair size 13 (9mm) needles OR SIZE TO OBTAIN GAUGE

Red scarf
- *Isis*, 3¹⁄₂oz/100g hanks, each approx 108yd/100m (viscose): 1 hank in #61 earth (A)
- *Zanziba*, 3¹⁄₂oz/100g hanks, each approx 98yd/88m (wool/viscose): 1 hank in #71 fire (B)
- One pair size 17 (12.75mm) needles OR SIZE TO OBTAIN GAUGE

Gold scarf
- *Isis*, 3¹⁄₂oz/100g hanks, each approx 108yd/100m (viscose): 2 hanks in #102 plerro
- One pair size 10 (6mm) needles OR SIZE TO OBTAIN GAUGE

Dark blue scarf
- *Isis*, 3¹⁄₂oz/100g hanks, each approx 108yd/100m (viscose): 2 hanks in #93 lapis
- One pair size 10 (6mm) needles OR SIZE TO OBTAIN GAUGE

SIZES
One size fits all.

SEED STITCH
(over an odd number of sts)
Row 1 (RS) *K1, p1; rep from *, end k1.
Rep row 1 for seed st.

LIGHT BLUE SCARF

FINISHED MEASUREMENTS
- Approx 8" x 40"/20.5cm x 101.5cm (without fringe)

GAUGE
8 sts and 18 rows to 4"/10cm over pat st.
TAKE TIME TO CHECK YOUR GAUGE.

Note Scarf is knit sideways.

PATTERN STITCH
Row 1 (RS) K with A.
Row 2 (WS) K with A.
Row 3 P with A.
Row 4 K with A.
Row 5 K with B.
Row 6 P with B.
Rep rows 1 to 6 for pat st.

SCARF
With B, loosely cast on 78 sts. K 2 rows. Work 6 rows pat st 5 times, then rep rows 1 to 4 once (6 ridges in A). **Next row (RS)** K 2 rows B. Bind off loosely.

Twisted cord fringe
With A, cut 38"/96.5cm long. Fold in half and knot end. Hold one end in each hand and twist in opposite directions. Fold in half and let twist upon itself. Knot open end. Attach to scarf as foll: with crochet hook, pull knotted end through scarf. Now draw knotted end through folded end and pull tight. Place fringe at every ridge on short end of scarf.

RED SCARF

FINISHED MEASUREMENTS
- Approx 7" x 48"/17.5cm x 122cm (without tassels)

GAUGE
7.5 sts and 10 rows to 4"/10cm over seed st.
TAKE TIME TO CHECK YOUR GAUGE.

Notes
1 One strand of A and B are held tog throughout.
2 Wind off 4yd/3.7m of A and B for tassels before beg.

SCARF
With A and B held tog, cast on 13 sts. Work in seed st for 48"/122cm. Bind off.

Tassels
Cut A and B 11"/28cm long. Mix colors and make 2 tassels. Gather each short end of scarf
(Continued on page 138)

Feet First
for intermediate knitters

Treat their feet with colorful cotton socks. Designed by Lila P. Chin, these striped sensations are a cinch to stitch and match the sweaters on page 60. "Feet First" first appeared in the Spring/Summer '98 issue of *Family Circle Easy Knitting* magazine.

MATERIALS

Teal/lime socks

- *Cotton Sox* by Classic Elite Yarns, .88oz/25g bags, each approx 69yd/62m (cotton) 1 bag each in #4977 teal (A) and #4935 lime (B)
- One set (4) size 2 (2.5mm) double pointed needles (dpn) OR SIZE TO OBTAIN GAUGE

Orange/goldenrod socks

- *Cotton Fleece* by Brown Sheep Co., 3½oz/100g balls, each approx 215yd/197m (cotton/wool)
- 1 ball each in #310 wild orange (A) and #340 goldenrod (B)
- One set (4) size 4 (3.5mm) double pointed needles OR SIZE TO OBTAIN GAUGE

GAUGE

29 sts and 40 rnds to 4"/10cm over St st using size 2 (2.5mm) needles.
TAKE TIME TO CHECK YOUR GAUGE.

CUFF

Beg at top edge with A, on one needle cast on 48 sts. Divide sts on three needles with 16 sts on each needle. Join, taking care not to twist sts on needles. Mark end of rnds and sl marker every rnd. Work around in k2, p2 rib for 2"/5cm.

Beg stripe pat

Change to St st and stripe pat as foll: 8 rnds B, 4 rnds A, 1 rnd B, 4 rnds A (17 rnds). Cont in stripe pat, rep these 17 rnds, until leg measures approx 6¼"/16cm from beg, end with 8 rnds B.

HEEL

With A, k 12 from first needle, then sl last 12 sts from 3rd needle onto other end of the same needle—24 heel sts. Divide rem 24 sts onto two needles to be worked later for instep. With MC, work back and forth in rows on heel sts only as foll: **Row 1 (WS)** Sl 1 purlwise, p to end. **Row 2** *Wyib, sl 1 purlwise, k1; rep from 0 to end. Rep these 2 rows until heel piece measures 1"/2.5cm, end with a p row. Turn heel.

Next row (WS) Sl 1, pl2, p2tog, p1, turn. **Row 2**

Sl 1, k3, SKP, k1, turn. **Row 3** Sl 1, p4, p2tog, pl, turn. **Row 4** Sl 1, k5, SKP, k1, turn. Cont in this way always having 1 more st before dec and SKP on RS rows, p2tog on WS rows until all sts have been worked—14 sts rem.

Shape instep

Next rnd With same needle and cont with A, pick up and k 11 sts along side of heel piece (*Needle 1*); with *Needle 2*, k next 24 sts (instep); with *Needle 3*, pick up and k 11 sts along other side of heel piece, with same needle, k 7 sts from first needle—60 sts. Mark center of heel for end of rnd. Resume working stripe pat as before. **Rnd 1** *Needle 1*, k to last 3 sts, k2tog, kl; *Needle 2*, knit; *Needle 3*, k1, SKP, k to end. **Rnd 2** Knit. Rep last 2 rnds 5 times more—48 sts. Cont stripe pat, work even until foot measures 4 (5, 6)"/10 (12.5, 15.25) cm or 1½"/4cm less than desired length from back of heel to end of toe.

Shape toe

Rnd 1 *Needle 1*, k to last 3 sts, k2tog, k1; *Needle 2*, k1, SKP, k to last 3 sts, k2tog, k1; *Needle 3*, k1, SKP, k to end. **Rnd 2** Knit. Rep last 2 rnds 4 times more—28 sts. Place 14 sts on 2 needles and weave tog using Kitchener st.

FINISHING

Block socks, omitting ribbing.

ORANGE/GOLDENROD SOCKS

GAUGE

24 sts and 32 rnds to 4"/10cm over St st using size 4 (3.5mm) needles.
TAKE TIME TO CHECK YOUR GAUGE.

CUFF

Beg at top edge with A, on one needle cast on 36 sts. Divide sts on three needles with 12 sts on each needle. Join, taking care not to twist sts on needles. Mark end of rnds and sl marker every rnd. Work around in k2, p2 rib for 2"/5cm.

Beg stripe pat

Change to St st and stripe pat as foll: 6 rnds B, 2 rnds A, 1 rnd B, 2 rnds A (11 rnds). Rep these 11 rnds for stripe pat, until leg measures approx 6¼"/16cm from beg, end with 3rd complete 11-rnd rep.

HEEL

With A, k9 from first needle, then sl last 9 sts from 3rd needle onto other end of same needle—18 heel sts. Divide rem 18 sts onto 2 needles to be worked later for instep. With A, work back and forth in rows on heel sts only as

(Continued on page 138)

Stripe it Rich
for intermediate crocheters

Cheerful bands of color liven up a stocking cap. Simple rows of crochet stitches craft this winter favorite, from the Cleckheaton Design Studio. "Stripe it Rich" first appeared in the Winter '99/'00 issue of *Family Circle Easy Knitting* magazine.

MATERIALS
- *Cleckheaton Country 8 Ply* by Plymouth, 1³/₄oz/50g balls, each approx 105yd/96m (wool)
  2 balls in #1979 purple (MC)
  1 ball each in #1860 iris (A) and #1548 blue (B)
- Size F/5 (4mm) crochet hook OR SIZE TO OBTAIN GAUGE

SIZES
One size fits all.

FINISHED MEASUREMENTS
- Head circumference 22"/56cm
- Length 20"/50cm

GAUGE
19 sts and 20 rows to 4"/10cm over pat st, using a F/5 (4mm) crochet hook.

Pattern stitch
*4 rnds sc, 1 rnd dc; rep from * (5 rnds) for pat st.

STRIPE PATTERN
*3 rnds B, 2 rnds A, 3 rnds MC, 2 rnds B, 3 rnds A, 2 rnds MC; rep from * (15 rnds) for stripe pat.

HAT
Beg at top, with B, ch 4. Join with sl st to first ch to form ring. Work in pat st and stripe pat as foll:

Foundation rnd Ch 1, work 5 sc in ring, join with sl st to first st at end of this and every rnd.

Rnd 1 Sc in each sc.

Rnd 2 Work 2 sc in each sc—10 sc.

Rnd 3 Sc in each sc.

Rnd 4 Ch 3 (counts as 1 dc), sk first sc, dc in each of next 9 sc—10dc.

Rnd 5 Dc in first st, *2sc in next st, sc in next st; rep from * to last st, 2 sc in last st—15sc.

Rnds 6 and 7 Sc in each sc.

Rnd 8 Sc in next 2 sc, *2 sc in next sc, sc in next 2 sc; rep from * to last sc, 2 sc in last sc—20 sc.

Rnds 9 and 10 Work even.

Rnd 11 Sc in next 3 sc, *2 sc in next sc, sc in 3 sc; rep from * to last sc, 2 sc in last sc—25sc.

Rnds 12-14 Work even.

Rnd 15 Sc in next 4 dc, *2 sc in next dc, sc in next 4 dc; rep from * to last st, 2 sc in last dc—30 sc. Cont in this way to inc 5 sts every 4th rnd until there are 100 sts. Work 13 rnds even, end with 3 rnds sc and MC. Fasten off.

FINISHING

Tassel
With MC, wind yarn 8 times around a piece of cardboard 4"/10cm long to make tassel. Attach to top of hat. (See page 90)

Antarctic Treasures

for intermediate knitters

Who wouldn't love these cuddly cuties? Designed by Jenny Bellew, this easy-to-knit trio of stuffed penguins is sure to bring smiles when the holidays roll around. "Antarctic Treasures" first appeared in the Winter '98/'99 issue of *Family Circle Easy Knitting* magazine.

MATERIALS

- *Cleckheaton Country 8-Ply* by Plymouth, 1¾oz/50g skeins, each approx 105yd/96m (wool)
  2 skeins in #0006 black (MC) and 1 skein in #0003 white (C1)
  Small amounts of #1857 gold (C2) and #1884 yellow (C3)
- One pair size 3 (3mm) needles OR SIZE TO OBTAIN GAUGE
- ⅜"/10mm sew-on eyes
- Fiberfill

FINISHED MEASUREMENTS

- 12"/30cm tall

GAUGE

28 sts and 38 rows to 4"/10cm over St st with MC using size 3 (3mm) needles.
TAKE TIME TO CHECK YOUR GAUGE.

BODY

BACK

With MC, cast on 5 sts. K 1 row, p 1 row.
Row 3 Inc 1 st, k to last 2 sts, inc 1 st, k1—7 sts.
Row 4 and all WS rows Purl.
Rows 5 and 7 Rep row 3.
Row 9 [Inc 1 st, k2] 3 times, inc 1 st, k1—15 sts.
Rows 11, 15, and 19 Rep row 3.
Row 13 [Inc 1 st, k4] 3 times, inc1 st, k1—21 sts.
Row 17 [Inc 1 st, k6] 3 times, inc 1 st, k1—27 sts.
Row 21 [Inc 1 st, k8] 3 times, inc 1 st, k1—33 sts.
Cont to work in St st, rep row 3 every 4 rows until 39 sts. Work 35 rows even. Mark each end of last row for position of flippers.
Next row K1, [k2tog, k3] 4 times, [SKP, k3] 3 times, SKP, k1—31 sts. Work 3 rows even.
Next row K1, [k2tog, k2] 3 times, k2tog, k1, [SKP, k2] 3 times, SKP, k1—23 sts. Work 3 rows even.
Head shaping
Next row K6, [inc in next st, k2] 3 times, inc in next st, k7—27 sts. P 1 row.
Note To turn, bring yarn to front of work, sl 1, yarn to back of work, sl same st back to LH needle, then turn work.
Rows 79 and 80 Work to last 4 sts, turn.
Rows 81 and 82 Work to last 8 sts, turn.
Rows 83 and 84 Work even in St st on all sts. Rep last 6 rows 4 more times.
Row 109 K1, k2tog, k4, k2tog, k9, SKP, k4, SKP, k1.
Row 110 and all WS rows Purl.
Row 111 K1, k2tog, k3, k2tog, k7, SKP, k3, SKP, k1.
Row 113 K1, k2tog, k2, k2tog, k5, SKP, k2, SKP, k1.
Row 115 K1, k2tog, k1, k2tog, k3, SKP, k1, SKP, k1—11 sts. Cast on 3 sts for beak.
Row 117 K4, [k2tog] twice, k1, [SKP] twice, k1, turn, cast on 3 sts—13 sts.
Row 119 Knit.
Row 121 K5, sl 2, k1, p2sso, k5—11 sts.
Row 123 K4, sl 2, k1, p2sso, k4—9 sts.
Row 125 K3, sl 2, k1, p2sso, k3—7 sts.
Row 127 K2, sl 2, k1, p2sso, k2—5 sts.
P 1 row. Cut yarn, leaving a long end. Draw end through rem sts and gather tightly tog. Fasten off. Sew beak seam.

FRONT

With C1, cast on 5 sts. Work as for body back through row 7. Cont in St st, inc as in row 3 every other row once, every 4th row twice—17 sts. P 1 row.
Row 19 K3, bind off 3 sts for leg opening, k5, bind off 3, k3.
Row 20 P3, turn; cast on 6 sts, turn; p5 turn; cast on 6 sts, turn; p3—23 sts. Cont in St st, inc as in row 3 at each end of next and foll 4th row—27 sts. Work 25 rows even.
Dec row 51 K1, k2tog, k to last 3 sts, SKP, k1. Rep dec row every 6 rows 3 times—19 sts. Work 3 rows even.
Row 73 [K1, k2tog] 3 times, [k1, SKP] 3 times, k1—13 sts.
Work 3 rows even.
Next row K4, turn; p4.
Next row K across all sts.
Next row P4, turn; k4.
Next row P across all sts.
Rep last 4 rows twice. Cont in St st, rep row 51 every other row 4 times—5 sts. Work 1 row even. Bind off.
With MC, duplicate st underside of neck and face. With C3, duplicate st from top of flippers to underside of neck. With C4, duplicate st a few places randomly on chest. (See photo) Sew front body to back, with bound-off sts of front body at cast-on sts of beak, leaving an opening for stuffing. Stuff firmly, finish sewing closed.

FEET (make 2)

With MC, cast on 6 sts. ***Beg with a k row, work 4 rows in St st.
Row 5 *[Insert needle into next st and into corresponding lp of cast-on edge and k these
(Continued on page 139)

Cover Girl
for intermediate knitters

Chase the chill with fashion finesse. Cascades of cables, courtesy of the Cleckheaton Design Studio, are just lovely in pale lavender. "Cover Girl" first appeared in the Winter '99/'00 issue of *Family Circle Easy Knitting* magazine.

MATERIALS
- *Cleckheaton Country 8 ply* by Plymouth, 1³/₄oz/50g balls, each approx 105yd/96m (wool) in #1980 lilac
- Hat: 2 balls; Scarf: 6 balls; Gloves: 2 balls
- One pair size 6 (4mm) needles OR SIZE TO OBTAIN GAUGE
- One set size 6 (4mm) dpn
- Cable needle

SIZES
Shown in one size.

FINISHED MEASUREMENTS
Hat
- Head circumference 22"/56cm

Scarf
- Width 8"/20cm
- Length 63"/160cm

GAUGE
22 sts and 30 rows to 4"/10cm over St st using size 6 (4mm) needles.
TAKE TIME TO CHECK YOUR GAUGE.

STITCHES USED
C7B
Sl 4 sts to cn and hold to back, k3, k4 from cn.
C6B
Sl 3 sts to cn and hold to back, k3, k3 from cn.
C5B
Sl 3 sts to cn and hold to back, k2, k3 from cn.
C4B
Sl 2 sts to cn and hold to back, k2, k2 from cn.

HAT
Cast on 110 sts. Divide sts evenly onto 3 dpn. Join, taking care not to twist sts. Mark end of rnd and sl marker every rnd. P 3 rnds, inc 16 sts evenly across last rnd—126 sts.

Beg cable pat
Rnds 1-4 *P2, k7; rep from * around.
Rnd 5 *P2, C7B; rep from * around.

Rnds 6-8 Rep rnd 1.
Rep rnds 1-8 for 42 rnds more.

Shape crown
Rnd 1 *P2, k2tog, k5; rep from * around—112 sts.
Rnd 2 *P2, C6B; rep from * around.
Rnd 3 *P2, k6; rep from * around.
Rnd 4 *P2, k2tog, k4; rep from * around—98 sts.
Rnd 5 *P2, k5; rep from * around.
Rnd 6 *P2tog, k5; rep from * around—84 sts.
Rnd 7 *P1, k5; rep from * around.
Rnd 8 *P1, C5B; rep from * around.
Rnd 9 *P1, k2tog, k3; rep from * around—70 sts.
Rnd 10 *P1, k4; rep from * around.
Rnd 11 *K2tog, k3; rep from * around—56 sts.
Rnd 12 and every other rnd Knit.
Rnd 13 *K2tog, k2; rep from * around—42 sts.
Rnd 15 *K2tog, k1; rep from * around—28 sts.
Rnd 17 K2tog around—14 sts.
Rnd 19 K2tog around—7 sts.
Break yarn, thread through rem sts, draw up and fasten off securely.

SCARF
Cast on 56 sts. K 1 row, p 1 row, k 1 row, inc 14 sts evenly across last row—70 sts.

Beg edge pat
Row 1 (RS) *K6, p2; rep from * to last 6 sts, k6.
Rows 2-4 K the knit sts and p the purl sts. Row 5 *C6B, p2; rep from * to last 6 sts, C6B.
Rows 6-8 Rep row 2.
Rep rows 1-8 for pat for 15 rows more.

Next row (WS) Work 8 sts, [p2tog p2] 5 times, p2tog, work 10 sts, p2tog, [p2tog, p2] 5 times, work 8 sts—58 sts.

Beg main pat
Row 1 K6, p2, k16, p2, k6, p2, k16, p2, k6. Rows 2-4 K the knit sts and p the purl sts.
Row 5 C6B, p2, k16, p2, C6B, p2, k16, p2, C6B.
Rows 6-8 Rep row 2.
Rep rows 1-8 for pat until piece measures approx 59"/151cm from beg, end with row 7.
Next row (WS) Work 8 sts, [inc in next st, p2] 5 times, inc in next st, work 10 sts, inc in next st, [inc in next st, p2] 5 times, work 8 sts—70 sts. Work 24 rows of edge pat as before, dec 14 sts evenly across last row—56 sts. Work 3 rows rev St st. Bind off loosely knitwise.

GLOVES

RIGHT GLOVE
Cast on 42 sts. K 1 row, p 1 row, k 1 row, inc 16 sts evenly across last row—58 sts.
Beg pat
Row 1 (RS) P2, *k6, p2; rep from * to end. **Rows 2-4** K the knit sts and p the purl sts.
Row 5 P2, *C6B, p2; rep from * to end.
Rows 6-8 Rep row 2.
Rep rows 1-8 for pat for 16 rows more, dec 13 sts evenly across last row—45 sts. Cont to work all sts in St st as foll: Work 2 rows even.**

(Continued on page 138)

Ballet Class

for intermediate knitters

Dress your budding ballerina in this pretty-in-pink set designed by Linda Cyr. A row of crochet gathers up the tulle skirt; the bodice is simply picked up and knit from there. Top it off with a whisper-soft surplice-wrap sweater and matching leg warmers. "Ballet Class" first appeared in the Fall '97 issue of *Family Circle Knitting* magazine.

MATERIALS

Surplice

■ *Deluxe Baby DK* by Jarol/Plymouth 1¾oz/50g balls, each approx 170yd/153m (acrylic/nylon)

    4 (4, 5, 6) skeins in #2201 pink

■ One pair each sizes 2 and 4 (2.75 and 3.5mm) needles OR SIZE TO OBTAIN GAUGE

■ Size F/5 (4mm) crochet hook

■ Stitch marker

■ 1½yd/1.4m of ⅞"/22mm-wide-double faced satin ribbon in pink

■ Sewing needle and thread

Leg warmers

■ *Deluxe Baby DK* by Plymouth 1¾oz/50g balls, each approx 170yd/153m (acrylic/ nylon)

    3 (3, 4, 4) skeins in #2201 pink

■ One pair each sizes 2 and 4 (2.75 and 3.5mm) needles OR SIZE TO OBTAIN GAUGE

■ 1yd/.95m in pink *Rainbow Elastic*™ by K1C2 Solutions

■ Tapestry needle

SIZES

Sized for Child's 2 (4, 6, 8). Shown in size 2.

FINISHED MEASUREMENTS

■ Chest 22 (24½, 27, 29½)"/56 (62, 68.5, 75)cm

■ Length 11¼ (13, 14½, 15½)"/28.5 (33, 37, 39.5)cm

■ Width at upper arm 9 (10, 10½, 11¾)"/23 (25.5, 26.5, 30)cm

GAUGE

23 sts and 31 rows to 4"/10cm over St st, using size 4 (3.5mm) needles.
TAKE TIME TO CHECK GAUGE.

STITCHES USED

Ssk Sl 2 sts knitwise, one at a time, to RH needle. Insert LH needle into fronts of these 2 sts and k2tog from this position.

Ssp Sl 2 sts knitwise, one at a time, to RH needle; sl these sts back to LH needle; inserting RH needle first through 2nd, then first st, p these 2 sts tog through back loops.

BACK

With smaller needles, cast on 63 (71, 77, 85) sts. Work in k1, p1 rib for 6 rows. Change to larger needles. Work in St st for 38 (46, 52, 56) rows. Piece measures approx 5¾ (6¾, 7½, 8)"/14.5 (17, 19, 20.5)cm from beg.

Raglan armhole shaping

Bind off 2 (3, 3, 4) sts at beg of next 2 rows. **Next (dec) row (RS)** K1, k2tog, k to last 3 sts, ssk, k1. Rep dec row every other row 3 (5, 5, 7) times more, then alternately [every 4th row once, every 2nd row once] 4 (4, 5, 5) times—35 (37, 39, 41) sts. Work 1 row even. Armhole measures 4¼ (5, 5¾, 6¼)"/10.5 (12.5, 14.5, 16)cm.

Neck shaping

Next row (RS) K9, join 2nd skein and bind off center 17 (19, 21, 23) sts, work to end. Working both sides of neck at same time, work as foll: **Next row** P9; on 2nd half, bind off 3 sts, p to end. **Next row** K1, k2tog, k3; on 2nd half, bind off 3 sts, k to last 3 sts, ssk, k1. **Next row** P5; on 2nd half, bind off 3 sts, p to end. **Next row** K2; on 2nd half, bind off 3 sts, k to end. Bind off rem 2 sts each side.

RIGHT FRONT

Cast on and work ribbing as for back. Change to larger needles. Working in St st, work 1 row even. **Next row (WS)** P to last 3 sts, ssp, p1. **Next row** K1, ssk, k to end. Rep last 2 rows 12 (11, 9, 10) times more—37 (47, 57, 63) sts. Cont to work decs on RS rows only, AT SAME TIME, when same length as back to underarm, shape right raglan armhole as for back until 3 sts rem, end with a WS row. **Next row (RS)** K3tog. Fasten off last st.

LEFT FRONT

Work to correspond to right front, reversing shaping as foll: **Next row (WS)** P1, p2tog, p to end. **Next row** K to last 3 sts, k2tog, k1. When

(Continued on page 139)

Crochet Cool

Your kids will love these super looks that are tops in crocheted chic.

Bathing Beauties

for beginner crocheters

Airy mesh ponchos, designed by Veronica Manno, are sure to make a big summer splash. Crocheted in cool colors in two easy rectangles, they whip up in no time. "Bathing Beauties" first appeared in the Spring/Summer '01 issue of *Family Circle Easy Knitting* magazine.

MATERIALS

Pink poncho

- *Sugar 'n Cream Sport* by Lily®, 1¾oz/50g balls, each approx 125yd/114m (cotton) 3 balls in #12 pink
- Size H/8 (5mm) crochet hook OR SIZE TO OBTAIN GAUGE

Coral poncho

- *Sugar 'n Cream Sport* by Lily®, 1¾oz/50g balls, each approx 125yd/114m (cotton) 3 (4, 4) balls in #7 coral
- One pair size 8 (5mm) knitting needles OR SIZE TO OBTAIN GAUGE
- Size 8 (5mm) circular needle 16"/40cm long
- One size 10 (6mm) knitting needle for binding off neck
- Size H/8 (5mm) crochet hook
- Stitch marker

PINK PONCHO

SIZES

Sized for one size to fit child's 4 to 8.

FINISHED MEASUREMENTS

- Approx 32"/81cm wide by 21"/53cm long (measured at longest point)

GAUGE

4 sts to 4"/10cm and 6 rows to 6½"/16.5cm over mesh pat using H/8 (5mm) crochet hook. TAKE TIME TO CHECK YOUR GAUGE.

MESH PATTERN

Ch a multiple of 4 plus 2.

Row 1 (RS) Work 1 sc into 2nd ch from hook, ch 6, sk 3 ch, sc into next ch; rep from * to end. Turn.

Row 2 Ch 8 (counts as 1 tr and ch 3), 1 sc into first ch-6 sp, *ch 6, 1 sc in next ch-6 sp; rep from *, end ch 3, 1 tr in last sc, turn.

Row 3 Ch 1, 1 sc into first tr, *ch 6, 1 sc into next ch-6 sp; rep from *, end working last sc into 5th ch of beg ch from previous row.

Rep rows 2 and 3 for mesh pat.

Rectangles (Make 2)

Ch 50. Work in mesh pat for 20"/50.5cm. Fasten off.

FINISHING

Block pieces lightly. Sew foundation ch edge of one piece along 12"/30.5cm of side of other piece. Sew the other seam in reverse.

NECKBAND

Work 3 rnds of sc evenly around neck edge, skipping 1 st at each v-point.

Along lower edge of poncho, work 1 rnd sc and 1 rnd backwards sc (from left to right).

CORAL PONCHO

SIZES

Sized for child's 4 (6, 8). Shown in size 4.

FINISHED MEASUREMENTS

- Approx 28 (30, 32)"/71 (76, 81)cm wide by 13 (14, 15)"/33 (35.5, 38)cm long (measured at longest point, without fringe)

GAUGE

14 sts and 12 rows to 4"/10cm over pat st using 8 (5mm) needles.

TAKE TIME TO CHECK YOUR GAUGE.

KERCHIEF

With straight needles, cast on 2 sts.

Row 1 (RS) K1, yo, k1.

Row 2 P3.

Row 3 *K1 tbl, yo; rep from *, end k1 tbl.

Row 4 P1 and k1 into back of same st (for inc), p4—6 sts.

Row 5 K1 tbl, yo, *k2tog tbl, yo; rep from *, end k1 tbl—7 sts.

Row 6 P1 and k1 into back of same st (for inc), p to end.

Row 7 K1 tbl, yo, *k2tog tbl, yo; rep from *, end k1 tbl.

Rep rows 6 and 7 until there are 53 sts, or to desired width, end with a row 7. Bind off loosely purlwise on WS. Do not cut yarn. Cont with crochet hook in last st, place last st on hook and ch 35 for tie, turn. Sc in 2nd ch from hook and in each ch to end, cont sc along edge of kerchief to other side, ch 35 for tie, turn, sc in 2nd ch from hook and in each ch to end. Cut yarn and pull through last lp.

(Continued on page 141)

Carefree Comfort

for intermediate crocheters

From study sessions to slumber parties, Mari Lynn Patrick's plush pullovers make dynamite coverups. Featuring rows of double crochet and stripes of a two-color stitch pattern, they're extra comfy in plush chenille yarn. "Carefree Comfort" first appeared in the Fall '99 issue of *Family Circle Easy Knitting* magazine.

MATERIALS

Blue Colorway

▪ *Chenille Sensations* by Lion Brand 1.4oz/40g balls, each approx 87yd/80m (acrylic)
   9 (9, 10, 10) balls in #111 blue (A)
   7 (7, 8, 8) balls in #145 violet (B)
   3 (3, 4, 4) balls in #140 raspberry (C)
   4 (4, 5, 5) balls in #147 purple (D)

Brick Colorway

▪ 9 (9, 10, 10) balls in #143 brick (A)
   7 (7, 8, 8) balls in #140 raspberry (B)
   3 (3, 4, 4) balls in #145 violet (C)
   4 (4, 5, 5) balls in #153 black (D)

▪ Size H/8 (5mm) crochet hook OR SIZE TO OBTAIN GAUGE

FINISHED MEASUREMENTS

▪ Bust 42 (45, 47, 49)"/106.5 (114, 119, 124.5)cm
▪ Length 24 (24½, 25, 25)"/61 (62, 63.5, 63.5)cm
▪ Upper arm 17 (18, 18½, 19)"/43 (46, 47, 48)cm

GAUGE

14 hdc and 12 rows to 4"/10cm over hdc pat st using size H/8 (5mm) crochet hook.
TAKE TIME TO CHECK YOUR GAUGE

Notes

1 When changing to a new color at beg of a row, pull new color through last 3 lps of previous row to complete last hdc and ch 2, turn with new color.
2 Ch 2 for turning does not count as 1 hdc.
3 Pat is reversible, so be sure that slant pat always slants to the left when foll the chart on RS or WS.

BACK

With size H/8 (5mm) crochet hook and A, ch 78 (82, 86, 90). **Row 1** Work 1 hdc in 3rd ch from hook and in each ch to last ch, pulling B through last 3 lps on hook, ch 2 turn. There are 76 (80, 84, 88) hdc. Then cont in hdc, work in stripe pat as foll: 8 rows B, 4 rows C, 1 row D, 2 rows slant pat foll chart with B and D, 11 rows A, 2 rows slant pat with C and D, 1 row D, 5 rows A, 6 rows B, 2 rows D, 1 row C, 2 rows D, 6 rows B, 1 row D, 2 rows slant pat with C and D, 11 rows A, 2 rows slant pat with B and D, 1 row D, 3 (4, 6, 6) rows A. Piece measures approx 24 (24½, 25, 25)"/61 (62, 63.5, 63.5)cm from beg. Fasten off.

FRONT

Work as for back until piece measures approx 21 (21½, 22, 22)"/53 (54.5, 56, 56)cm from beg, end with 8th (9th, 11th, 11th) row in last 11-row stripe in A.

Neck shaping

Next row Work 28 (30, 32, 34) hdc, leave rem sts unworked. Working on first side of neck only, dec 1 hdc by [yo and draw up a lp in next hdc] twice, yo and through all 5 lps on hook, then work to end. Cont to dec 1 hdc at neck edges every row 5 times more—22 (24, 26, 28) hdc. Work even for 3 more rows. Fasten off. Skip center 20 sts for neck and work other side of neck to correspond.

SLEEVES

With size H/8 (5mm) crochet hook and D, ch 33 (35, 37, 37). Working in hdc pat on 31 (33, 35, 35) hdc, work in stripe pat of 1 row D, 6 rows B, 2 rows D, 1 row C, 2 rows D, 6 rows B, 5 rows A, 1 row D, 2 rows slant pat with C and D, 11 rows A, 2 rows slant pat with B and D, 1 row D, 4 rows C, 8 rows B, AT SAME TIME, inc 1 st each side every 6th row 1 (1, 1, 0) time, every 3rd row 14 (14, 14, 16) times—61 (63, 65, 67) hdc. Work even in stripe pat until piece measures 18"/45.5cm from beg. Fasten off.

COLLAR

With size H/8 (5mm) crochet hook and A, ch 92. Working on 90 hdc, work in stripe pat of 7 rows A, 1 row D, 2 rows slant pat with C and D, 11 rows A, 2 rows slant pat with B and D, 1 row D, 4 rows C, AT SAME TIME shape collar by dec 4 hdc evenly every other row once, dec 6 hdc evenly every other row twice, then inc 6 hdc
(Continued on page 141)

Hip to be Square
for intermediate crocheters

Revamp seventies' chic. Mari Lynn Patrick's retro-inspired knee-length skirt is crocheted in a kaleidoscope of funky granny squares edged in black. "Hip to be Square" first appeared in the Spring/Summer '01 issue of *Family Circle Easy Knitting* magazine.

MATERIALS

■ *Microspun* by Lion Brand Yarn Co., 2¹⁄₂oz/70g balls, each approx 168yd/154m (acrylic)
  2 (2, 3) balls in #153 black (MC)
  1 ball each in #98 vanilla, #100 white, #148 turquoise, #194 lime, #47 purple, #113 red, #158 yellow, #144 lilac, #186 orange, #101 pink, #103 coral and #146 dk. pink
■ One each sizes F/5 (4mm) and G/6 (4.5mm) crochet hooks OR SIZE TO OBTAIN GAUGE
■ 1 yd/.95m of ¹⁄₂"/13mm wide black elastic

SIZES
Sized for Small (Medium, Large) Shown in size Small.

FINISHED MEASUREMENTS
■ Waist 28 (30, 32)"/71 (76, 81)cm
■ Hip 34¹⁄₂ (38¹⁄₂, 42¹⁄₂)"/87.5 (98, 108)cm
■ Length 22¹⁄₂"/57cm

GAUGE
Square measures 4"/10cm using size G/6 (4.5mm) hook.
TAKE TIME TO CHECK YOUR GAUGE.

Notes
1 Each square is made using an alternating color for each rnd (A, B, C or D) with colors used in different combinations.
2 MC is used to crochet squares tog from the RS with progressively larger chains between joining at the lower edge of skirt for a slight flare at the hem.

SQUARE (make 40 (45, 50)
Beg at center with A and size G/6 (4.5mm) hook, ch 6, join with sl st to first ch to form ring.
Rnd 1 With A, ch 3 (counts as 1 dc), work 15 dc in ring, join with sl st to top of ch-3. Fasten off.
Rnd 2 With B, make a lp on hook, work 1 dc in any dc, ch 2, *dc in next dc, ch 2; rep from * around, join with sl st to top of first dc. Fasten off.
Rnd 3 With C, make a lp on hook, work 2 dc in any ch-2 sp for beg corner, *ch 1 [2 dc in next sp, ch 1] 3 times, ch 3 for corner, 2 dc in next sp, rep from *, end ch 3, join to top of first dc at corner. Fasten off.
Rnd 4 With D, make a lp on hook, work 1 sc in each dc and ch-1 sp around, working 4 sc in each corner sp; join and fasten off.

FINISHING
Block pieces lightly to measurements. Schematic shows layout for size Small only, but for layout of squares for all sizes, work 4 (4¹⁄₂, 5) squares across for front or back and 5 squares down for all sizes. Join squares in rows foll schematic as foll: **Row 1** With MC and size F/5 (4mm) hook, join with sl st in one corner of first square, ch 2, join in corresponding corner of second square with sl st, *ch 2, skip 1 sc and sl st in next sc on first square, ch 2, skip 1 sc and sl st in next sc on second square; rep from * along one straight edge to join 2 squares. Cont to join squares across in this way until there is a total of 8 (9, 10) squares joined for row 1, and waist of skirt.
Rows 2 and 3 Work as for row 1.
Row 4 Work as for row 1, only work ch 3 instead of ch 2 in between each sl st.
Row 5 Work as for row 1, only work ch 4 instead of ch 2 in between each sl st. Then join all 5 strips tog to form one piece, working square joining for row 1. Join piece tog at final seam working joinings as for rows 1-5 with longer progressive chains.

LOWER EDGE
With size G/6 (4.5mm) hook and MC, join in one seam and *ch 3, sc in 2nd ch from hook, ch 2, skip 1 sc, sl st in next sc; rep from * around lower edge, join in first sl st and fasten off.

WAISTBAND
Rnd 1 With size G/6 (4.5mm) hook and MC, join in one side seam, * sc in each of 2 sc along top edge, draw up a lp in each of next 2 sc, yo and through all 3 lps on hook (to dec 1 sc); rep from * around top edge counting each joining as 1 sc, join to first sc.
Rnd 2 Ch 5, work 1 tr in each sc around. Fasten off. Cut elastic to fit waistband and sew in circle. Fold waistband in half to WS and sew over waistband.

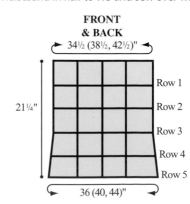

FRONT & BACK
34¹⁄₂ (38¹⁄₂, 42¹⁄₂)"
21¹⁄₄"
Row 1
Row 2
Row 3
Row 4
Row 5
36 (40, 44)"

Mari Lynn Patrick's daisy-stitched cardigans are all a-bloom. Both are ultra-easy to make; take your pick from a graceful cardigan or fashion-forward bolero style. "Two Sweet" first appeared in the Fall '99 issue of *Family Circle Easy Knitting* magazine.

MATERIALS

- *Cuddle Soft* by Caron International, 1¾oz/50g skeins, each approx 202yd/186m (acrylic)

Shorter version
  6 (7) skeins in #2747 lavender

Longer version
  7 (8) skeins in #2701 white

- Size G/6 (4.5mm) crochet hook OR SIZE TO OBTAIN GAUGE

FINISHED MEASUREMENTS

- Bust (closed) 34½ (41)"/87.5 (104)cm
- Length
  Shorter version 13½ (15)"/34 (38)cm
  Longer version 16 (17½)"/40.5 (44.5)cm
- Upper arm 13 (15)"/33 (38)cm

GAUGE

3 floral pat groups to 6½"/16.5cm, 6 rows to 4"/10cm over floral pat st using size G/6 (4.5mm) hook.
TAKE TIME TO CHECK YOUR GAUGE.

FLORAL PATTERN STITCH

(Ch a multiple of 8 sts plus 4)

Row 1 °° Yo hook twice, insert hook into ch and draw up a lp, yo and draw through 2 loops, yo and draw through 2 loops (for a double tr) °°, work between °°'s 2 more times for a total of 3 times into 8th ch from hook, yo and through 4 lps on hook, *ch 7, rep between °°'s 3 times as before into same ch, yo and through 4 lps on hook, ch 3, skip 3 ch, 1 dc in next ch, ch 3, skip 3 ch, rep between °°'s 3 times in next ch, yo and through 4 lps on hook*; rep between *'s ending with ch 3, dc in last ch. Turn at end of this and every row.

Row 2 Ch 3, rep between °°'s 3 times in first ch-3 sp, yo and through 4 lps on hook, *ch 3, rep between °°'s twice into top of cluster just worked, yo and through 3 lps on hook, work 1 dc in 4th ch of next ch-7 arc, ch 3, rep between °°'s twice into same st as dc just worked, then rep between °°'s 3 times in the next ch-3 sp, then rep between °°'s 3 times into next ch-3 sp before pat group, yo and through all 9 lps on hook*, rep between *'s, end with rep between °°'s 3 times in last ch, yo and through all 6 lps on hook.

Row 3 Ch 3, rep between °°'s twice into top of first cluster, yo and through 3 lps on hook, *ch 3, dc in next dc, ch 3, rep between °°'s 3 times into center of next cluster pat group, yo and through all 4 lps on hook, ch 7, rep between °°'s 3 times into center of same cluster pat group as before, yo and through all 4 lps on hook*, rep between *'s, ending just before a ch-7.

Row 4 Ch 7, rep between °°'s twice in 4th ch from hook, *rep between °°'s 3 times into next ch-3 sp, rep between °°'s 3 times into next ch-3 sp before next pat group, yo and through all 9 loops on hook, ch 3, rep between °°'s twice into top of cluster pat group just worked, yo and through all 3 loops on hook, 1 dc in 4th ch of next ch-7 arc, ch 3, rep between °°'s twice into same st as dc just worked*, rep between *'s, end with double tr into ch at edge.

Row 5 *Ch 3, rep between °°'s 3 times into center of next cluster pat group, yo and through all 4 loops on hook, ch 7, rep between °°'s 3 times in same center st as before, yo and through 4 loops on hook, ch 3, dc in next dc *, rep between *'s, end 1 dc in edge.
Rep rows 2-5 for pat st.

Note
End with pat rows 2 or 4 when finishing off.

BODY

Beg at lower edge with size G/6 (4.5mm) hook and chosen color, ch 132 (156). Work in floral pat st on 16 (19) floral pat groups until piece measures 5½"/14cm OR 8 rows from beg for shorter version and 8"/20.5cm or 12 rows from beg for longer version. For both versions, end with pat row 4.

Separate for back and fronts
Skip first 4 (5) floral pat groups (right front), rejoin yarn and pat across next 8 (9) floral pat groups (back), leave last 4 (5) floral pat groups unworked (left front).

BACK

Cont to work on these 8 (9) floral pat groups for back for 10 (12) rows more, end with pat row 2 (4). Armhole measures approx 6½ (8)"/16.5 (20.5)cm. Fasten off for back.

RIGHT FRONT

Rejoin yarn from RS to work across first 4 (5) floral pat groups and beg with pat row 5, work in pat st for 6 more rows, end with pat row 2. Cut yarn.

(Continued on page 141)

Square Deal

for beginner crocheters

You go, girls! Mari Lynn Patrick's hooded granny-square pullovers, in two different lengths, boast a simple floral design and flower-trimmed ties. A matching bag featuring double crochet straps totes her treasures. "Square Deal" first appeared in the Fall '99 issue of *Family Circle Easy Knitting* magazine.

MATERIALS

- *Red Heart® Soft* by Coats & Clark, 5oz/140g skeins, each approx 328 yd/302m (acrylic)
  Shorter version
  4 skeins in #7769 fuchsia (MC) and 3 skeins in #7001 white (CC)
  Longer version
  4 skeins in #7722 lt rose (MC) and 3 skeins in #7001 white (CC)
- Sizes G/6 and H/8 (4.5 and 5mm) crochet hooks OR SIZE TO OBTAIN GAUGE

Bag

- *Red Heart® Soft* in 1 skein each in #7773 med pink (A), #7322 gold (B), #7821 med blue (C), #7815 lt blue (D), #7664 blue green (B-2), #7775 dk rose (C-2) and #7722 lt pink (D-2)
- *TLC® by Red Heart®* by Coats & Clark, 5oz/140g skeins, each approx 253yd/233m (acrylic)
  1 skein in #5657 kiwi (A-2)
- Sizes G/6 and H/8 (4.5 and 5mm) crochet hooks, OR SIZE TO OBTAIN GAUGE

SIZES

Sized for Small (Medium) in 2 different lengths. Shown in size Medium.

FINISHED MEASUREMENTS

- Bust 34 (42)"/86 (106.5)cm
- Length
  Shorter version 21"/53cm
  Longer version 25½"/64.5cm
- Upper arm 17"/43cm

GAUGE

Square measures 4"/10cm before edge in CC and 4½"/11.5cm after edge in CC using size H/8 (5mm) hook.
TAKE TIME TO CHECK YOUR GAUGE.

Note

Schematic is drawn to represent Medium size, shorter version.

GRANNY SQUARE

Beg at center with size H/8 (5mm) hook and CC, ch 4, join with a sl st in first ch to form ring. **Rnd 1** Ch 3 (counts as 1 dc), 2 dc in ring, ch 2, [3 dc, ch 2] 3 times in ring. Join with sl st to top of ch-3. Fasten off CC. **Rnd 2** Rejoin (MC) with sl st into one ch-2 corner sp and ch 3, 2 dc in same sp, ch 2, 3 dc in same sp, *ch 1, 3 dc, ch 2 and 3 dc in next ch-2 sp; rep from * twice more, ch 1, join with sl st in top of ch-3. **Rnd 3** Skip 1 dc and sl st in next dc then sl st in next ch-2 sp, ch 3, 2 dc in same sp, ch 2, 3 dc in same sp, *ch 1, 3 dc in ch-1 sp, ch 1, 3 dc, ch 2 and 3 dc in corner ch-2 sp; rep from * twice more, ch 1, 3 dc in ch-1 sp, ch 1, join with sl st to top of ch-3. **Rnd 4** Skip 1 dc and sl st in next dc, then sl st in next ch-2 sp, ch 3, 2 dc in same sp, ch 2, 3 dc in same sp, *[ch 1, 3 dc in ch-1 sp] twice, ch 1, 3 dc, ch 2 and 3 dc in corner ch-2 sp; rep from * twice more, [ch 1, 3 dc in ch-1 sp] twice, ch 1, join with sl st to top of ch-3. Fasten off MC. **Rnd 5** Rejoin CC in one corner and work 3 sc in each ch-2 corner, 1 sc in each dc and 1 sc in each ch-1 sp around. Join with sl st to first sc and fasten off.

For small size, shorter version

For back, make 20 squares. For front, make 20 squares. For each sleeve make 13 squares.

For small size, longer version

For back and front make 24 squares each and 13 squares for each sleeve.

For medium size, shorter version

For back and front, make 20 squares each. In addition, make 6 more squares to fold in half at side seams. For each sleeve, make 13 squares.

For medium size, longer version

For back and front, make 24 squares each. In addition, make 8 more squares to fold in half at side seams. For each sleeve, make 13 squares.

HOOD

For hood on all sizes and both versions, make 11 squares.

FINISHING

Foll schematic for placement, sew 20 (24) squares tog for back sewing from RS through inside lps only (leave outside lps free). Sew 20 (24) squares tog for front only do not sew squares 2 and 3 tog at center front for front neck slit (see schematic). Sew squares 1 and 4 tog for shoulder seams on front and back. For medium size, sew 6 (or 8) more squares at front side seams foll schematic, fold in half and sew to back side seams. For sleeves, sew 12 squares tog foll schematic then
(Continued on page 142)

Crochet Cool

Knits for Kids Basics

A bright cheerful palette, easy stitches and plenty of whimsical embellishments make knitting for kids rewarding and so much fun. There is nothing more gratifying than presenting a hand knit sweater to a little one and having the recipient thank you with a smile. In *Family Circle Easy Knits for Kids*, you'll find an appealing array of projects children will love! From simple accessories to traditional and sophisticated knits, this spirited collection of knits for kids packs more than fifty of our favorite styles from past issues.

Whether you want to knit the captivating ladybug pullover or a rough-and-tumble sweater for your little man, you're sure to find something to suit every season, preference and occasion. In addition, we've updated many of the yarns for your convenience, but don't let that stop you from exploring your creative side and experimenting with new yarns and textures. The results may just surprise you!

Your children's measurements are constantly changing during the growing years, so be sure to measure your child before you begin knitting to determine which size to make. Whether you're looking for a playful penguin pullover or a breezy crocheted summer poncho, you'll find the perfect pattern for small fry in this delightful assortment of unforgettable designs.

GARMENT CONSTRUCTION

Even though most of the garments in this book are made in pieces, if you are a fairly experienced knitter, you can try knitting many of them in the round, or pick up your sleeve stitches at the underarms and work down to the cuff. You just need to make some simple adjustments to the pattern.

SIZING

Since clothing measurements have changed in recent decades, it is important to measure your child to determine which size to make.

YARN SELECTION

For an exact reproduction of the projects photographed, use the yarn listed in the "Materials" section of the pattern. We've chosen yarns that are readily available in the U.S. and Canada at the time of printing. The Resources list on pages 143 provides addresses of yarn distributors. Contact them for the name of a retailer in your area.

YARN SUBSTITUTION

You may wish to substitute yarns. Perhaps you view small-scale projects as a chance to incorporate leftovers from your yarn stash, or the yarn specified may not be available in your area. You'll need to knit to the given gauge to obtain the knitted measurements with a substitute yarn (see "Gauge" below). Be sure to consider how the fiber content of the substitute yarn will affect the comfort and the ease of care of your projects.

After you've successfully gauge-swatched a substitute yarn, you'll need to figure out how much of the substitute yarn the project requires. First, find the total length of the original yarn in the pattern (multiply number of balls by yards/meters per ball). Divide this figure by the new yards/meters per ball (listed on the ball band). Round up to the next whole number. The answer is the number of balls required.

FOLLOWING CHARTS

Charts are a convenient way to follow colorwork, lace, cable, and other stitch patterns at a glance. FCEK stitch charts utilize the universal knitting language of "symbolcraft." When knitting back and forth in rows, read charts from right to left on right side (RS) rows and from left to right on wrong side (WS) rows, repeating any stitch and row repeats as directed in the pattern. When knitting in the round, read charts from right to left on every round. Posting a self-adhesive note under your working row is an easy way to keep track of your place on a chart.

LACE

Lace knitting provides a feminine touch. Knitted lace is formed with "yarn overs," which create an eyelet hole in combination with decreases that create directional effects. To make a yarn over (yo), merely pass the yarn over the right-hand needle to form a new loop. Decreases are worked as k2tog, ssk, or SKP depending on the desired slant and are spelled out specifically with each instruction. On the row or round that follows the lace or eyelet detail, each yarn over is treated as one stitch. If you're new to lace knitting, it's a good idea to count the stitches at the end of each row or round. Making a gauge swatch in the stitch pattern enables you to practice the lace pattern. Instead of binding off the swatch, place the final row on a holder, as the bind off tends to pull in the stitches and distort the gauge.

COLORWORK KNITTING

Two main types of colorwork are explored in this book.

INTARSIA

Intarsia is accomplished with separate bobbins of individual colors. This method is ideal for large blocks of color or for motifs that aren't repeated close together. When changing colors, always pick up the new color and wrap it around the old color to prevent holes.

GAUGE

It is still important to knit a gauge swatch to assure a perfect fit in a sweater. If the gauge is incorrect, a colorwork pattern may become distorted. The type of needles used—straight, circular, wood or metal—will influence gauge, so knit your swatch with the needles you plan to use for the project. Measure gauge as illustrated here. (Launder and block your gauge swatch before taking measurements). Try different needle sizes until your sample measures the required number of stitches and rows. To get fewer stitches to the inch/cm, use larger needles; to get more stitches to the inch/cm, use smaller needles. It's a good idea to keep your gauge swatch to test any embroidery or embellishment, as well as blocking, and cleaning methods.

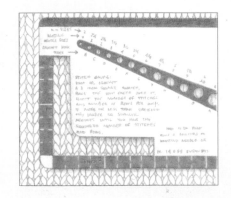

TWISTED CORD

1 If you have someone to help you, insert a pencil or knitting needle through each end of the strands. If not, place one end over a doorknob and put a pencil through the other end. Turn the strands clockwise until they are tightly twisted.

2 Keeping the strands taut, fold the piece in half. Remove the pencils and allow the cords to twist onto themselves.

STRANDING

When motifs are closely placed, colorwork is accomplished by stranding along two or more colors per row, creating "floats" on the wrong side of the fabric. This technique is sometimes called Fair Isle knitting after the traditional Fair Isle patterns that are composed of small motifs with frequent color changes.

To keep an even tension and prevent holes while knitting, pick up yarns alternately over and under one another across or around. While knitting, stretch the stitches on the needle slightly wider than the length of the float at the back to keep work from puckering.

When changing colors at the beginning of rows or rounds, carry yarn along for a few rows only, or cut yarn and rejoin when needed. It is important to keep the "floats" small and neat so they don't catch when pulling on the piece.

BLOCKING

Blocking is an all-important finishing step in the knitting process. It is the best way to shape pattern pieces and smooth knitted edges in preparation for sewing together. Most garments retain their shape if the blocking stages in the instructions are followed carefully. Choose a blocking method according to the yarn care label and when in doubt, test-block your gauge swatch.

WET BLOCK METHOD

Using rust-proof pins, pin pieces to measurements on a flat surface and lightly dampen using a spray bottle. Allow to dry before removing pins.

STEAM BLOCK METHOD

With WS facing, pin pieces. Steam lightly, holding the iron 2"/5cm above the knitting. Do not press or it will flatten stitches.

FINISHING

The pieces in this book use a variety of finishing techniques. Directions for making fringes are on page 124. Also refer to the illustrations such as "Invisible Seaming: Stockinette St" for other useful techniques.

HAND-SEWING

Several items in this book require hand-sewing in the finishing. Use a fine point hand sewing needle and sewing thread that matches the color of the trim. Cut the unsewn ends at an angle to prevent unraveling. When sewing on a trim, use back stitch and keep the stitches small and even.

CARE

Refer to the yarn label for the recommended cleaning method. Many of the projects in the book can be either washed by hand, or in the machine on a gentle or wool cycle, in lukewarm water with a mild detergent. Do not agitate, or soak for more than 10 minutes. Rinse gently with tepid water, then fold in a towel and gently press the water out. Lay flat to dry away from excess heat and light. Check the yarn band for any specific care instructions such as dry cleaning or tumble drying.

INVISIBLE SEAMING: STOCKINETTE ST

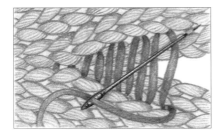

To make an invisible side seam in a garment worked in stockinette stitch, insert the tapestry needle under the horizontal bar between the first and second stitches. Insert the needle into the corresponding bar on the other piece. Pull the yarn gently until the sides meet. Continue alternating from side to side.

THE KITCHENER STITCH

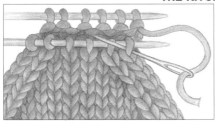

1 Insert tapestry needle purlwise (as shown) through first stitch on front needle. Pull yarn through, leaving that stitch on knitting needle.

2 Insert tapestry needle knitwise (as shown) through first stitch on back needle. Pull yarn through, leaving stitch on knitting needle.

3 Insert tapestry needle knitwise through first stitch on front needle, slip stitch off needle and insert tapestry needle purlwise (as shown) through next stitch on front needle. Pull yarn through, leaving this stitch on needle.

4 Insert tapestry needle purlwise through first stitch on back needle. Slip stitch off needle and insert tapestry needle knitwise (as shown) through next stitch on back needle. Pull yarn through, leaving this stitch on needle.
Repeat steps 3 and 4 until all stitches on both front and back needles have been grafted. Fasten off and weave in end.

DUPLICATE STITCH

Duplicate stitch covers a knit stitch. Bring the needle up below the stitch to be worked. Insert the needle under both loops one row above and pull it through. Insert it back into the stitch below and through the center of the next stitch in one motion, as shown.

WORKING A YARN OVER

There are different ways to make a yarn over. Which method to use depends on where you are in the stitch pattern. If you do not make the yarn over in the right way, you may lose it on the following row, or make a yarn over that is too big. Here are the different variations:

Between two knit stitches: Bring the yarn from the back of the work to the front between the two needles. Knit the next stitch, bringing the yarn to the back over the right-hand needle, as shown.

Between a knit and a purl stitch: Bring the yarn from the back to the front between the two needles. Then bring it to the back over the right-hand needle and back to the front again, as shown. Purl the next stitch.

Between a purl and a knit stitch: Leave the yarn at the front of the work. Knit the next stitch, bringing the yarn to the back over the right-hand needle, as shown.

Between two purl stitches: Leave the yarn at the front of the work. Bring the yarn to the back over the right-hand needle and to the front again, as shown. Purl the next stitch.

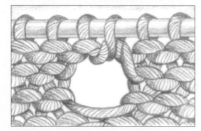

Multiple yarn overs (two or more): Wrap the yarn around the needle, as when working a single yarn over, then continue wrapping the yarn around the needle as many times as indicated. Work the next stitch of the left-hand needle. On the following row, work stitches into the extra yarn overs as described in the pattern. The illustration at right depicts a finished yarn-over on the purl side.

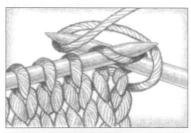

At the beginning of a knit row: Insert the right-hand needle knitwise into the first stitch on the left-hand needle, keeping the yarn in front of the needle. Bring the yarn over the right-hand needle to the back and knit the first stitch, holding the yarn over with your thumb if necessary.

At the beginning of a purl row: Insert the right-hand needle purlwise into the first stitch on the left-hand needle, keeping the yarn behind the needle. Purl the first stitch.

POMPOMS

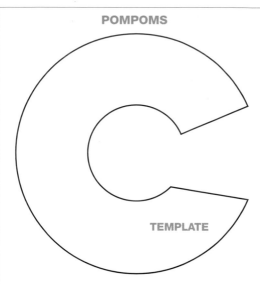

TEMPLATE

1 Following the template, cut two circular pieces of cardboard.

2 Hold the two circles together and wrap the yarn tightly around the cardboard several times. Secure and carefully cut the yarn.

3 Tie a piece of yarn tightly between the two circles. Remove the cardboard and trim the pompom to the desired size.

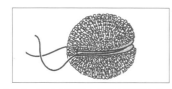

FRINGE

Simple fringe: Cut yarn twice desired length plus extra for knotting. On wrong side, insert hook from front to back through piece and over folded yarn. Pull yarn through. Draw ends through and tighten. Trim yarn.

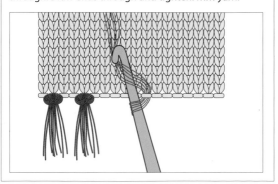

Knit/Crochet Terms and Abbreviations

approx approximately

beg begin(ning)

bind off Used to finish an edge and keep stitches from unraveling. Lift the first stitch over the second, the second over the third, etc. (UK: cast off)

cast on A foundation row of stitches placed on the needle in order to begin knitting.

CC contrast color

ch chain(s)

cm centimeter(s)

cont continu(e)(ing)

dc double crochet (UK: tr–treble)

dec decrease(ing)–Reduce the stitches in a row (knit 2 together).

dpn double-pointed needle(s)

dtr double treble (UK: trtr—triple treble)

foll follow(s)(ing)

g gram(s)

garter stitch Knit every row. Circular knitting: knit one round, then purl one round.

grp(s) group(s)

hdc half double crochet (UK: htr–half treble)

inc increase(ing)–Add stitches in a row (knit into the front and back of a stitch).

k knit

k2tog knit 2 stitches together

LH left-hand

lp(s) loop(s)

m meter(s)

M1 make one stitch–With the needle tip, lift the strand between last stitch worked and next stitch on the left-hand needle and knit into the back of it. One stitch has been added.

MC main color

mm millimeter(s)

no stitch On some charts, "no stitch" is indicated with shaded spaces where stitches have been decreased or not yet made. In such cases, work the stitches of the chart, skipping over the "no stitch" spaces.

oz ounce(s)

p purl

p2tog purl 2 stitches together

pat(s) pattern

pick up and knit (purl) Knit (or purl) into the loops along an edge.

pm place markers–Place or attach a loop of contrast yarn or purchased stitch marker as indicated.

psso pass slip stitch(es) over

rem remain(s)(ing)

rep repeat

rev St st reverse stockinette stitch–Purl right-side rows, knit wrong-side rows. Circular knitting: purl all rounds. (UK: reverse stocking stitch)

rnd(s) round(s)

RH right-hand

RS right side(s)

sc single crochet (UK: dc–double crochet)

sk skip

SKP Slip 1, knit 1, pass slip stitch over knit 1.

SK2P Slip 1, knit 2 together, pass slip stitch over the knit 2 together.

sl slip–An unworked stitch made by passing a stitch from the left-hand to the right-hand needle as if to purl.

sl st slip stitch (UK: sc–single crochet)

sp(s) space(s)

ssk slip, slip, knit–Slip next 2 stitches knitwise, one at a time, to right-hand needle. Insert tip of left-hand needle into fronts of these stitches from left to right. Knit them together. One stitch has been decreased.

sssk Slip next 3 sts knitwise, one at a time, to right-hand needle. Insert tip of left-hand needle into fronts of these stitches from left to right. Knit them together. Two stitches have been decreased.

st(s) stitch(es)

St st Stockinette stitch–Knit right-side rows, purl wrong-side rows. Circular knitting: knit all rounds. (UK: stocking stitch)

tbl through back of loop

t-ch turning chain

tog together

tr treble (UK: dtr—double treble)

trtr triple treble (UK: qtr—quadruple treble)

WS wrong side(s)

wyib with yarn in back

wyif with yarn in front

work even Continue in pattern without increasing or decreasing. (UK: work straight)

yd yard(s)

yo yarn over–Make a new stitch by wrapping the yarn over the right-hand needle. (UK: yfwd, yon, yrn)

* = Repeat directions following * as many times as indicated.

[ ] = Repeat directions inside brackets as many times as indicated.

KNITTING NEEDLES		CROCHET HOOKS	
US	METRIC	US	METRIC
0	2mm	14 steel	.60mm
1	2.25mm	12 steel	.75mm
2	2.5mm	10 steel	1.00mm
3	3mm	6 steel	1.50mm
4	3.5mm	5 steel	1.75mm
5	3.75mm		
6	4mm	B/1	2.00mm
7	4.5mm	C/2	2.50mm
8	5mm	D/3	3.00mm
9	5.5mm	E/4	3.50mm
10	6mm	F/5	4.00mm
10½	6.5, 7, 7.5mm	G/6	4.50mm
11	8mm	H/8	5.00mm
13	9mm	I/9	5.50mm
15	10mm	J/10	6.00mm
17	12.75mm		6.50mm
19	16mm	K/10½	7.00mm
35	19mm		

Fall Favorites

CLASS ACT

(Continued from page 10)

back edge. Work in St st for 4½"/11.5cm. Bind off all sts. With RS facing, smaller needles and MC, pick up and k16 sts between markers on front edge. Bind off all sts knitwise on WS. Place markers 7½ (8, 8½, 9)"/19 (20.5, 21.5, 23)cm down from shoulders on front and back for armholes. Sew sleeves between markers. Sew side seams, leaving opening for pockets. Sew sleeve seams. Sew zipper in position under front edging. Sew pocket linings to WS of front.

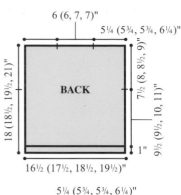

6 (6, 7, 7)"
5¼ (5¾, 5¾, 6¼)"
BACK
18 (18½, 19½, 21)"
7½ (8, 8½, 9)"
9½ (9½, 10, 11)"
1"
16½ (17½, 18½, 19½)"

5¼ (5¾, 5¾, 6¼)"
2½"
LEFT FRONT
7½ (8, 8½, 9)"
15½ (16, 17, 18½)"
9½ (9½, 10, 11)"
1"
8¼ (8¾, 9¼, 9¾)"

15 (16, 17, 18)"
SLEEVE
11 (11½, 12, 12½)"
1½"
8 (9, 9½, 10)"

Color Key

▲ Black (MC)

◉ Royal blue (A)

• Dusty blue (B)

Plaid Chart

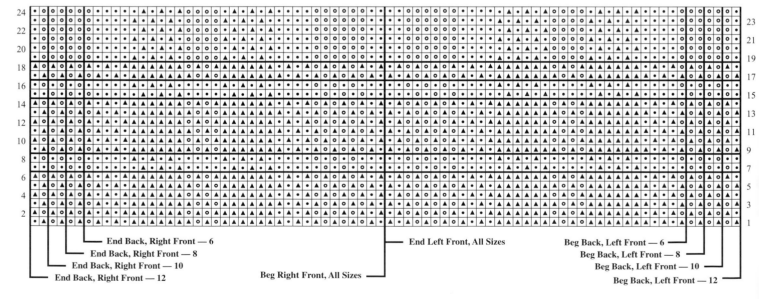

End Back, Right Front — 6
End Back, Right Front — 8
End Back, Right Front — 10
End Back, Right Front — 12

End Left Front, All Sizes

Beg Back, Left Front — 6
Beg Back, Left Front — 8
Beg Back, Left Front — 10
Beg Back, Left Front — 12

Beg Right Front, All Sizes

GIRL TALK

(Continued from page 12)

Turtleneck

With RS facing and smaller circular needle, pick up and k 64 (68, 72) sts evenly around neck edge. Join and work in k2, p2 rib for 2½"/6.5cm. Change to larger circular needle and cont rib for 2½"/6.5cm more. Bind off in rib.
Set in sleeves. Sew side and sleeve seams.

SHORT-SLEEVED PULLOVER

SIZES

Sized for Child's 6 (8/10, 12). Shown in size 8/10.

FINISHED MEASUREMENTS

■ Chest 30 (33, 36)"/76 (84, 91.5)cm
■ Length 17¾ (19¼, 20¾)"/45 (49.5, 53)cm
■ Upperarm 10½ (12, 13½)"/26.5 (30.5, 34.5)cm

GAUGE

18 sts and 24 rows to 4"/10cm over St st using larger needles.
TAKE TIME TO CHECK YOUR GAUGE.

BACK

With smaller needles, cast on 68 (74, 82) sts. Work in k1, p1 rib for 1"/2.5cm. Change to larger needles and work in St st until piece measures 11 (12, 12½)"/28 (30.5, 32)cm from beg.

Armhole shaping

Bind off 4 sts at beg of next 2 rows, dec 1 st each side every other row twice—56 (62, 70) sts. Work even until armhole measures 6 (6½, 7)"/15 (17, 19)cm.

Shoulder and neck shaping

Bind off 7 (8, 9) sts at beg of next 2 rows, 7 (8, 10) sts at beg of next 2 rows, AT SAME TIME, bind off center 18 (20, 22) sts for neck and working both sides at once, bind off 5 sts from each neck edge once.

FRONT

Work as for back until armhole measures 4¼ (4¾, 5¾)"/10.5 (12, 14.5)cm, end with a WS row.

Neck and shoulder shaping

Next row (RS) Work 22 (24, 27) sts, join 2nd ball of yarn and bind off center 12 (14, 16) sts, work to end. Working both sides at once, bind off from each neck edge 3 st once, 2 sts twice, 1 st once, AT SAME TIME, when same length as back to shoulder, shape shoulder as for back.

SLEEVES

With smaller needles, cast on 38 (42, 46) sts. Work in k1, p1 rib for 1"/2.5cm. Change to larger needles and work in St st, inc 1 st each side every other row 5 times, every 4th row 0 (1, 2) times—48 (54, 60) sts. Work even until piece measures 3½ (4½, 5)"/9 (11, 13)cm from beg.

Cap shaping

Bind off 4 sts at beg of next 2 rows, 3 sts at beg of next 2 rows, 2 sts at beg of next 2 rows, dec 1 st each side every other row 4 times, bind off 4 sts at beg of next 2 rows, 3 sts at beg of next 2 rows. Bind off rem 8 (14, 20) sts.

FINISHING

Block pieces to measurements. Sew shoulder seams.

Neckband

With RS facing and circular needle, pick up and k 72 (76, 80) sts evenly around neck edge. Join and work in k1, p1 rib for 1"/2.5cm. Bind off in rib. Set in sleeves. Sew side and sleeve seams.

TURTLENECK PULLOVER

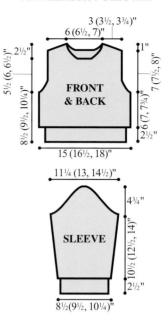

SHORT-SLEEVED PULLOVER

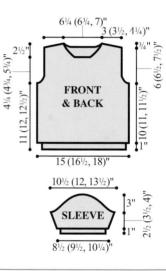

CHILD'S PLAY

(Continued from page 8)

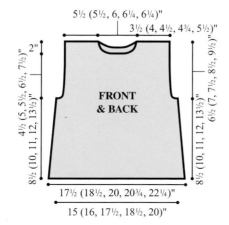

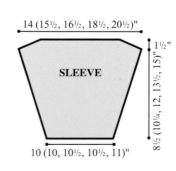

GREAT INVESTMENTS

(Continued from page 14)

center dec), rib to end. Rib 1 row even. Rep last 2 rnds until band measures ½"/1.5cm. Bind off in rib.

Armhole bands

With RS facing, circular needle and A, pick up and k 110 (120, 136) sts evenly around each armhole edge, Join and work in k1, p1 rib for ¾"/2cm. Bind off in rib.

Chart 1

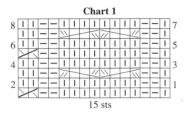

15 sts

Chart 2

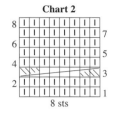

8 sts

Chart 3

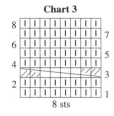

8 sts

Chart 4

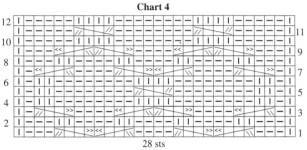

28 sts

Stitch Key

- ☐ K on RS, p on WS
- ⊟ P on RS, k on WS
- ⧅ 2-st RT
- ⧄ 4-st RC
- ⧅ 4-st LC
- << 4-st RPC
- >> 4-st LPC
- 8-st RC
- 8-st LC

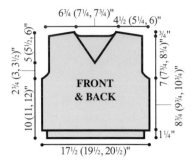

FRONT & BACK

ZIP IT UP!

(Continued from page 26)

Cap shaping
Note
Work 10 rows of chart 1 pat centered on same row as on back. Bind off 2 sts at beg of next 2 rows.

Dec row (RS) K1, SKP, k to last 3 sts, k2tog, k1. For right-hand edge (beg of RS rows), rep dec row every other row 13 (15, 17) times more, every 4th row 5 times, then bind off 5 sts from this edge every other row twice, 4 sts once; for left-hand edge (end of RS rows), rep dec row every other row 15 (17, 19) times more, every 4th row 6 times.

LEFT SLEEVE
Work as for right sleeve, reversing shaping at top of cap.

FINISHING
Block pieces lightly to measurements. Sew sleeves into raglan armholes.

HOOD
With larger needles and A, cast on 2 sts then pick up and k 95 (95, 101) sts evenly around neck including sts on holders, pm at center back st. On next row, cast on 2 sts and p to end on all 99 (99, 105) sts. Cont in St st for 1½"/4cm.
Inc row (RS) K to center mark st, M1, k1, M1, k to end. Rep inc row every 10th row 3 times

more—107 (107, 113) sts. Work even until hood measures 8½ (9, 9)"/21.5 (23, 23)cm, dec 1 st at center back marked st on last row—106 (106, 112) sts.

Dec row (RS) K to 3 sts before 2 center back neck sts, SKP, pm, k2, pm, k2tog, k to end. P1 row. Rep last 2 rows 7 times more—90 (90, 96) sts, end with a k row. Divide sts in half on 2 parallel needles with points at center p1 st tog from each needle while binding off to join hood at top. Sew side and sleeve seams. With smaller needles and A, pick up and k 80 sts evenly along center front edge. Bind off knitwise. Rep on other edge. Sew in zipper under front edge.

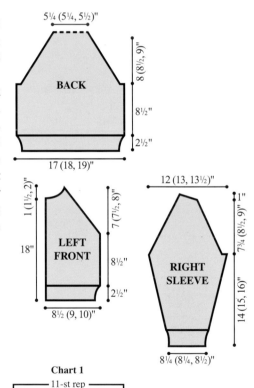

BACK

LEFT FRONT

RIGHT SLEEVE

Chart 2

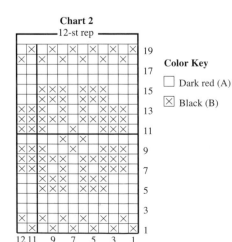

Color Key
- ☐ Dark red (A)
- ⊠ Black (B)

Chart 1

11-st rep

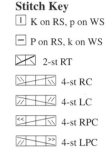

FARM FRESH

(Continued from page 28)

Small ear

With RS facing, larger needle and B, pick up 5 sts. Work in St st for 3 rows. Dec 1 st each side on next row. Work 2 rows even then bind off rem 3 sts.

Curly tail

With crochet hook and B, ch 10, turn and work 1 row sc. Fasten off and use ends to sew to back of pig.

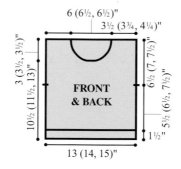

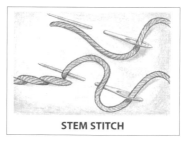

STEM STITCH

Color Key

- ☐ Blue (MC)
- ○ Brown (A)
- I Pink (B)
- + Pick-up for ear in pink (B)
- ◿ Dk. Brown (C)
- ☒ Pale green (D)
- △ Tan (E)
- ☓ Yellow (F)
- ■ Black (G)
- ● Black bead

Back Chart

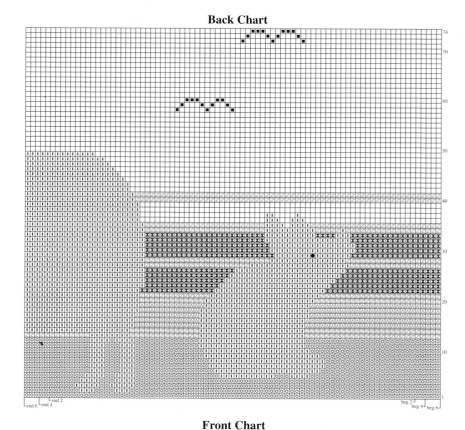

Front Chart

Winter Warmers

BOUCLÉ PULLOVER

(Continued from page 32)

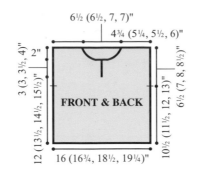

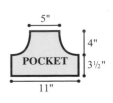

FAIR PLAY

(Continued from page 38)

Work 34 rows of Chart B. Work 4 rows Pat st.
Change to smaller needles. K 8 rows. Bind off.

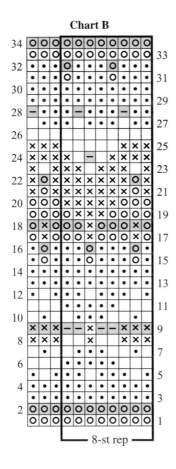

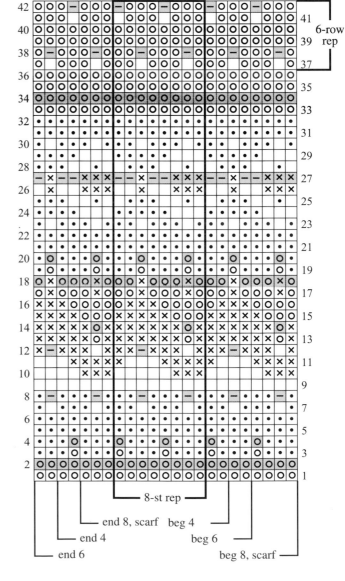

Chart B

Chart A

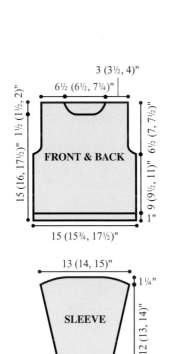

Color Key

k on RS, p on WS:
- ⊙ Grey (MC)
- ☐ White (A)
- ☒ Black (B)
- • Red or Blue (C)

p on RS, k on WS:
- ⊙ Grey (MC)
- − White (A)
- ☒ Black (B)

AFTERSCHOOL SPECIALS

(Continued from page 34)

each side to safety pins.

SLEEVES

With smaller needles and 1 strand A and B, cast on 25 (25, 27, 29) sts. Work in k1, p1 rib for 2"/5cm. Change to larger needles and work in St st inc 1 st each side every 4th row 11 (11, 12, 13) times—47 (47, 51, 55) sts. Work even until piece measures 12½ (13½, 15, 16)"/32 (34, 38, 40.5)cm from beg.

Raglan cap shaping

Bind off 2 sts at beg of next 2 rows.

Dec row (RS) K2, k3tog, k to last 5 sts, SK2P, k2. Rep dec row every 6th row 6 times, every 4th row 0 (0, 1, 2) times—15 sts. Work even, if necessary until sleeve cap fits into armhole. Sl rem sts to a holder.

FINISHING

Block pieces to measurements. Sew sleeves into armholes, leaving one seam open.

Turtleneck

With smaller needles and A and B held tog, pick up and k 80 (84, 84, 84) sts evenly around neck, including sts on holders. Work in k1, p1 rib for 7"/18cm. Bind off in rib. Sew other raglan and turtleneck seam, the last half with seam on RS for collar turnback. Sew side and sleeve seams.

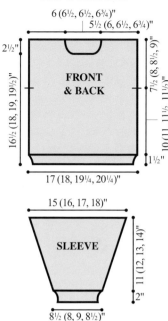

BOY'S SWEATER

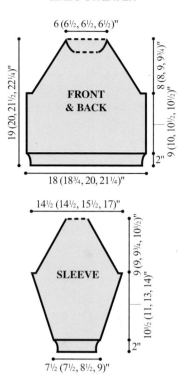

GIRL'S SWEATER

BEAR NECESSITY

(Continued from page 36)

Color Key

☐ MC

▦ A

⊡ B

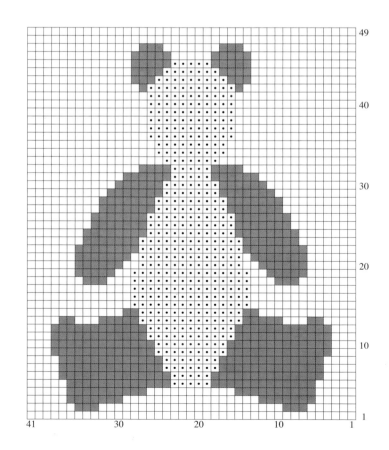

MULTIPLE CHOICE

(Continued from page 42)

SLEEVES

With A, cast on 32 (34, 34) sts. K 7 rows. Then work in Stripe pat, AT SAME TIME, inc 1 st each side on 3rd row, then every 4th row 9 (9, 12) times more, every 6th row 4 (6, 5) times—58 (64, 68) sts. Work even until piece measures 10³⁄₄ (12³⁄₄, 13³⁄₄)"/27.5 (32.5, 35)cm from beg. Bind off all sts.

FINISHING

Block pieces. Sew shoulder seams.

Collar

With WS facing and A, k 3 sts from left front holder, then with C, pick up and k14 (14, 15) sts along left front neck edge, 22 (26, 28) sts along back neck, 14 (14, 15) sts along right front neck edge, join A and k 3 from holder—56 (60, 64) sts. **Next row** K 3 with A, p50 (54, 58) with C, k 3 with A. **Next row** K3 A, k with C to last 3 sts, end k3 A. Cont in pat as established until collar measures 2"/5cm from beg, end with a p row. With A, k 4 rows on all sts. Bind off all sts loosely. Sew in zipper. Place markers 6¹⁄₂ (7, 7¹⁄₂)"/16.5 (18, 19)cm down from shoulders on front and back for armholes. Sew top of sleeves between markers. Sew side and sleeve seams.

GIRL'S SWEATER

Notes

1 When changing colors while working intarsia, bring new yarn under old to twist strands and prevent holes.

BACK

With A, cast on 64 (68, 72) sts. Beg with a WS row, k 7 rows. **Next row (RS)** K32 (34, 36) sts with B, join C and k to end. Cont in St st, matching colors, until piece measures 13 (15, 17)"/33 (38, 43)cm from beg, end with a WS row.

Shoulder shaping

Bind off 7 sts at beg of next 4 rows, 7 (7, 8) sts at beg of next 2 rows. Bind off rem 22 (26, 28) sts.

FRONT

Work as for back until piece measures 5 (7, 8³⁄₄)"/12.5 (18, 22)cm from beg, end with a WS row.

Placket shaping

Next row (RS) K 29 (31, 33), join A and k 6 sts, k with C to end. Cont in pat, working center 6 sts in garter st with A, for 5 rows more. Divide for zipper

opening: **Next row (RS)** K to center 6 sts, k3 with A, join 2nd skein of A and k3, k to end with C. Working both sides at once, work even until piece measures 11³⁄₄ (13³⁄₄, 15¹⁄₂)"/30 (35, 39.5)cm from beg, end with a WS row.

Neck shaping

Next row (RS) Work all sts of left front in pat; on right front, k3 with A and place these sts on a holder to be worked later, bind off next 4 sts, k in pat to end. **Next row** P to end of right front; on left front, place first 3 sts on a holder, bind off next 4 sts, p to end. Cont working both sides at once, dec 1 st at each neck edge every row 1 (3, 3) times, then every other row 3 (3, 4) times, AT SAME TIME, when same length as back to shoulders, shape shoulders each side as for back.

LEFT SLEEVE

With A, cast on 32 (34, 34) sts. K 7 rows. Then work in St st with D, inc 1 st each side on 3rd row, then every 4th row 9 (9, 12) times more, every 6th row 4 (6, 5) times—58 (64, 68) sts. Work even until piece measures 10³⁄₄ (12³⁄₄, 13³⁄₄)"/27.5 (32.5, 35)cm from beg. Bind off all sts.

RIGHT SLEEVE

With A, cast on 32 (34, 34) sts. K 7 rows. Then work in St st with F, working shaping as for left sleeve.

FINISHING

Block pieces. Sew shoulder seams.

COLLAR

With WS facing and A, k 3 sts from left front holder, then with E, pick up and k14 (14, 15) sts along left front neck edge, k 22 (26, 28) sts along back neck, 14 (14, 15) sts along right front neck edge, join A and k 3 from holder—56 (60, 64) sts. **Next row** K 3 with A, p50 (54, 58) with E, k 3 with A. **Next row** K3 A, k with E to last 3 sts, end k3 A. Cont in pat as established until collar measures 2"/5cm from beg, end with a p row. With A, k 4 rows on all sts. Bind off all sts loosely. Sew in zipper. Place markers 6¹⁄₂ (7, 7¹⁄₂)"/16.5 (18, 19)cm down from shoulders on front and back for armholes. Sew top of sleeves bet markers. Sew side and sleeve seams.

HAT

CAP

With A, beg at band edge by casting on 85sts, dividing evenly over 4 needles. Place marker

and join, being careful not to twist sts. **Rnd 1** Knits. **Rnd 2** Purl. **Rnds 3-6** Rep rnds 1 & 2, inc 5 sts evenly spaced on last rnd-90sts. **Next rnd** Change to B and work in St st for 2³⁄₄"/7cm from beg. **Next rnd** Change to A and k 2 rnds. **Next rnd** Change to C and *k10, pm; rep from * 9 times more. **Next rnd** *K8, k2tog; rep from * 9 times-81sts. **Next rnd** Knit. **Next rnd** *K7, k2tog; rep from * 9 times. **Next rnd** Knit. Cont to dec 1 st each panel in this way every other row until 1 st rem in each panel-9sts. Work 1 rnd, even, removing markers. **Next rnd** Cut yarn, leaving a long tail. Pull through sts to close and secure.

FINISHING

I-cord petals (make 5)

With C and dpn, cast on 4 sts. *K4, do not turn, push the stitches to the end of the needles and cont to k4 from beg until cord is 4"/10cm. Bind off, leaving a long tail. Make pompom. Arrange I-cords in circle by bending to form petals. Join ends of cord to form flower. Thread through top of crown with pompom and secure.

SCHEMATIC FOR BOY'S AND GIRL'S SWEATER

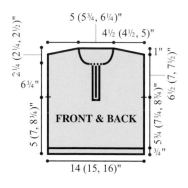

TWO OF A KIND

(Continued from page 48)

for 2"/5cm. Bind off in rib. With circular needle and B, pick up and k 43 sts along one side of front placket, 3 sts from safety pin, 43 sts along other side of placket. Bind off knitwise. Pin and baste zipper in place. Sew zipper into opening, so that zipper teeth extend beyond edge. Sew zipper securely in place at top and bottom, overcast edges on WS. Sew side and sleeve seams.

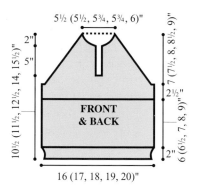

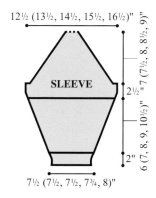

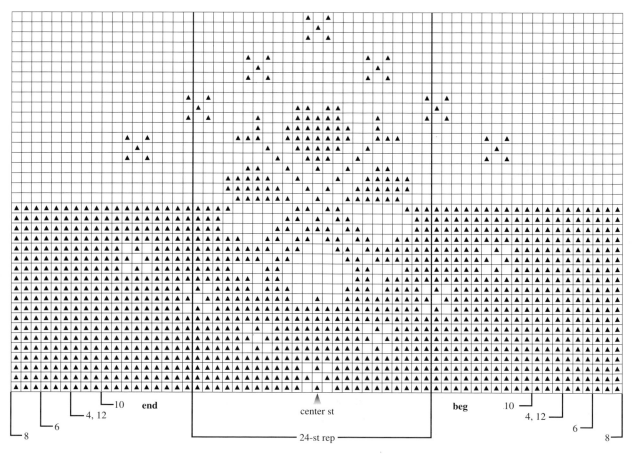

Summer Fun

HAPPY CAMPERS
(Continued from page 62)

BOY'S SWEATER

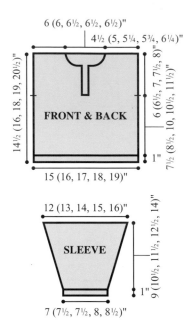

6 (6, 6½, 6½, 6½)"

4½ (5, 5¼, 5¾, 6¼)"

14½ (16, 18, 19, 20½)"

FRONT & BACK

6 (6½, 7, 7½, 8)"

7½ (8½, 10, 10½, 11½)"

1"

15 (16, 17, 18, 19)"

12 (13, 14, 15, 16)"

SLEEVE

9 (10½, 11½, 12½, 14)"

1"

7 (7½, 7½, 8, 8½)"

GIRL'S SWEATER

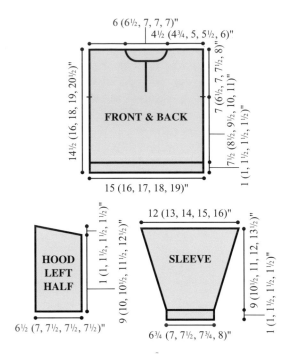

6 (6½, 7, 7, 7)"

4½ (4¾, 5, 5½, 6)"

14½ (16, 18, 19, 20½)"

FRONT & BACK

7 (6½, 7, 7½, 8)"

7 (6½, 9½, 10, 11)"

7½ (8½, 9½, 1½, 1½)"

1 (1, 1½, 1½, 1½)"

15 (16, 17, 18, 19)"

HOOD LEFT HALF

1 (1, 1½, 1½, 1½)"

1 (1, 10½, 11¼, 12½)"

6½ (7, 7½, 7½, 7½)"

12 (13, 14, 15, 16)"

SLEEVE

9 (10½, 11, 12, 13½)"

1 (1, 1½, 1½, 1½)"

6¾ (7, 7½, 7¾, 8)"

BUDDING BEAUTY
(Continued from page 66)

Stitch Key

☐ K on RS, P on WS

■ P on RS, K on WS

Chart 1

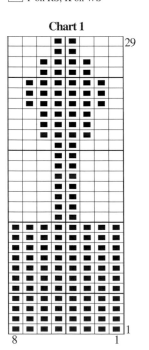

29

1

8   1

Chart 2

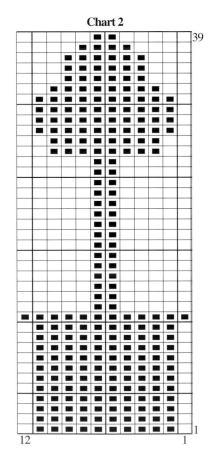

39

1

12   1

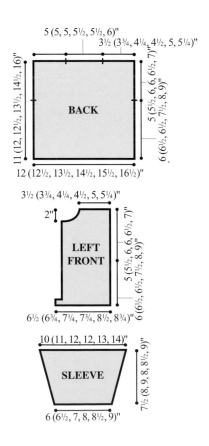

5 (5, 5, 5½, 5½, 6)"

3½ (3¾, 4¼, 4½, 5, 5¼)"

11 (12, 12½, 13½, 14½, 16)"

BACK

5 (5½, 6, 6, 6½, 7)"

6 (6½, 6½, 7½, 8, 9)"

12 (12½, 13½, 14½, 15½, 16½)"

3½ (3¾, 4¼, 4½, 5, 5¼)"

2"

LEFT FRONT

5 (5½, 6, 6, 6½, 7)"

6 (6½, 6½, 7½, 8, 9)"

6½ (6¾, 7¼, 7¾, 8½, 8¾)"

10 (11, 12, 12, 13, 14)"

SLEEVE

7½ (8, 9, 8, 8½, 9)"

6 (6½, 7, 8, 8½, 9)"

SUNFLOWER GIRL

(Continued from page 64)

Buttons

With crochet hook and A, ch 5, join with sl st to form ring. Place in center of plastic ring and with yarn underneath, work 16 sc into yarn ring and around plastic ring at same time. Fasten off. Sew to back shoulder.

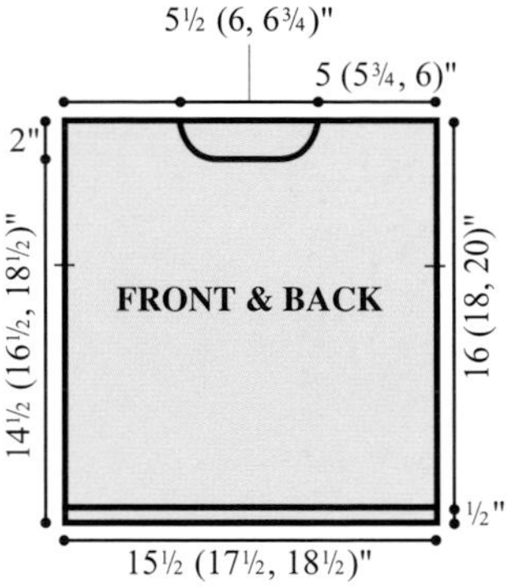
5½ (6, 6¾)"
5 (5¾, 6)"
2"
14½ (16½, 18½)"
FRONT & BACK
16 (18, 20)"
½"
15½ (17½, 18½)"

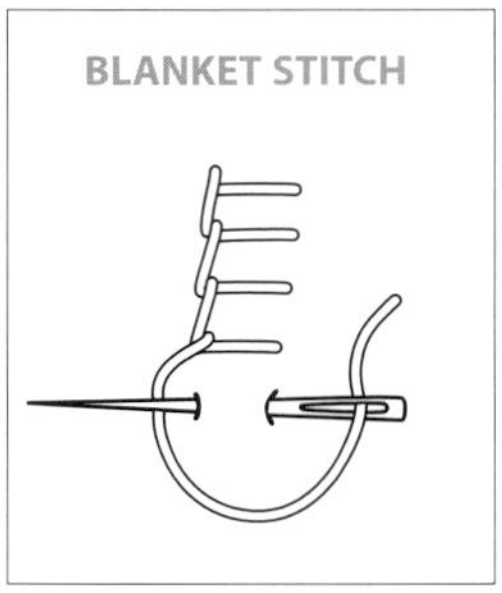
BLANKET STITCH

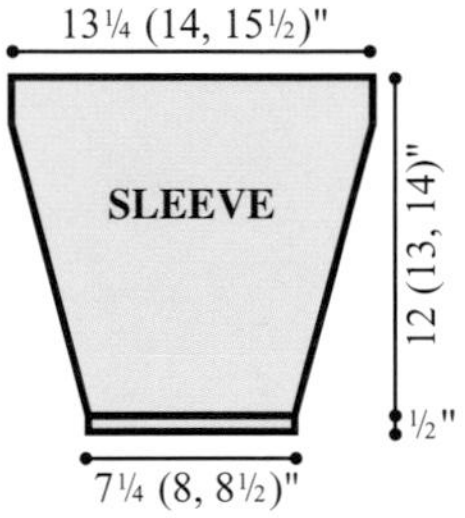
13¼ (14, 15½)"
SLEEVE
12 (13, 14)"
½"
7¼ (8, 8½)"

BUG OFF

(Continued from page 68)

stripe pat, inc 1 st each side every 4th row 3 times—72 (77, 82, 87) sts. Work even until piece measures 2"/5cm above turning ridge, end with a WS row.

Crotch shaping

Bind off 3 sts at beg of next 2 rows, 2 sts at beg of next 2 rows. **Next row (RS)** Dec 1 st, work to end. **Next row** Bind off 2 sts, work to end. Rep last 2 rows once more, then dec 1 st at beg of next WS row—55 (60, 65, 70) sts. Work even until piece measures 4 (4½, 5, 6)"/10 (11.5, 12.5, 15)cm from beg of crotch shaping, end with a RS row.

Drawstring hole

Next row (WS) Work to last 5 sts, p2tog, yo, p3. Work 2 rows more. Change to smaller needles. **Next row (RS)** (turning ridge) Purl, using same color as previous row. With B, work 5 rows in St st. Bind off. Work other leg to match, reversing shaping and drawstring placement.

FINISHING

Block pieces to measurements. Sew legs tog at center front and back. Sew leg seams. Turn hems to WS and sew in place.

Cord

With 3 strands MC, make twisted cord, approx 30 (34, 37, 40)"/76 (86.5, 94, 101.5)cm long. Knot cord 2"/5cm above each end of cord. Attach 4 beads onto each end.

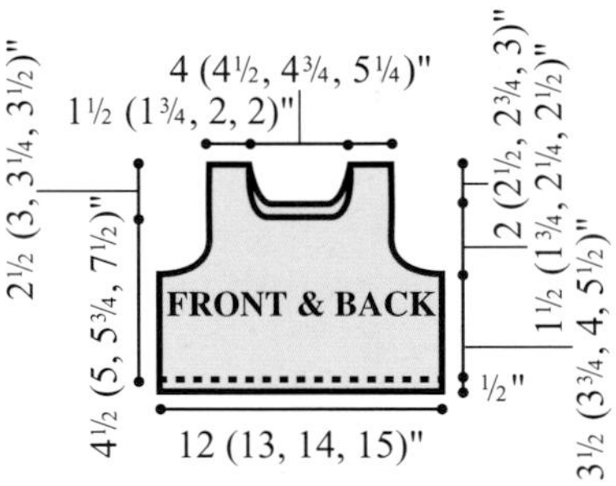
4 (4½, 4¾, 5¼)"
1½ (1¾, 2, 2)"
2½ (3, 3¼, 3½)"
4½ (5, 5¾, 7½)"
FRONT & BACK
2 (2½, 2¾, 3)"
1½ (1¾, 2¼, 2½)"
3½ (3¾, 4, 5½)"
½"
12 (13, 14, 15)"

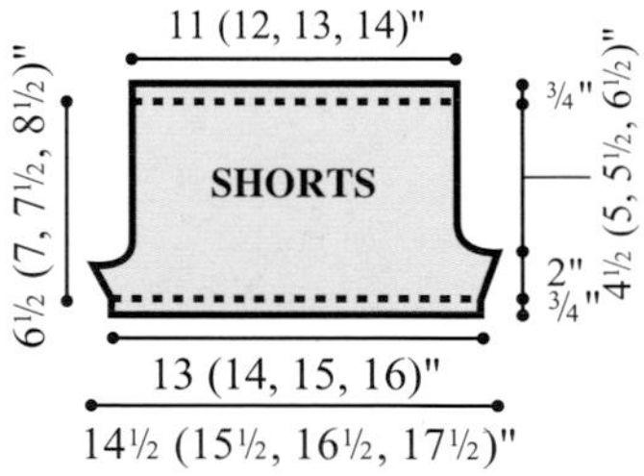
11 (12, 13, 14)"
¾"
SHORTS
4½ (5, 5½, 6½)"
2"
¾"
6½ (7, 7½, 8½)"
13 (14, 15, 16)"
14½ (15½, 16½, 17½)"

BEACH PATROL

(Continued from page 70)

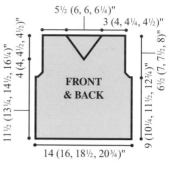

FRONT
& BACK

5½ (6, 6, 6¼)"

3 (4, 4¼, 4½)"

4 (4, 4¼, 4½)"

11½ (13¼, 14½, 16¼)"

9 (10¼, 11½, 12¾)"

6½ (7, 7½, 8)"

14 (16, 18½, 20¾)"

SLEEVE

12 (13, 14, 15)"

2½"

13 (14, 15, 16)"

7½"

Stitch Key

☐ K on RS, p on WS

◯ Yo

⊠ K2tog

⊠ SKP

⊠ SK2P

⊠ Duplicate st with A, B, C or D

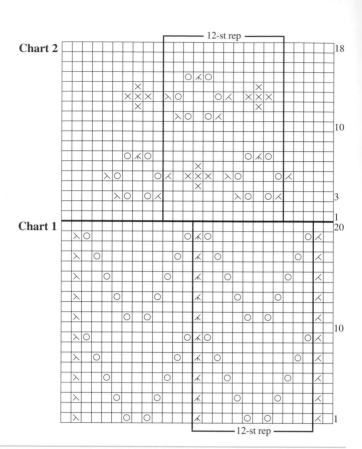

Chart 2

12-st rep

18

10

3

1

Chart 1

20

10

1

12-st rep

LIGHT AND LACY

(Continued from page 74)

6 sc, *[ch 3, sc in 3 sc] 3 times, sc in 3 sc; rep from * to end of last shell, then working up center right front for buttonloop band, work [ch 3, sc in 3 sc] 4 times, *ch 5 (for buttonloop), [sc in 3 sc, ch 3] twice, sc in 3 sc; rep from * twice more, ch 5 (last buttonloop), *sc in 3 sc, ch 3; rep from * for picot edge around neck to left shoulder. Join and fasten off. Sew buttons opposite buttonloops. Block again lightly if necessary.

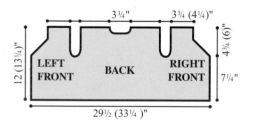

3¾"

3¾ (4¼)"

12 (13¼)"

4¾ (6)"

LEFT FRONT

BACK

RIGHT FRONT

7¼"

29½ (33¼)"

Stitch Key

☐ K on RS, p on WS

▬ P on RS, k on WS

◯ Yo

⊠ K2tog

⊠ Ssk

⊠ SK2P

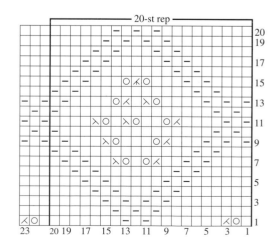

20-st rep

20
19
17
15
13
11
9
7
5
3
1

23 20 19 17 15 13 11 9 7 5 3 1

TICKLED PINK

(Continued from page 84)

and k 90 (94, 98) sts evenly around neck, including sts from holder. Beg with a p row, work in St st for 4 rows. Bind off purlwise on WS. Band will roll to outside.

Armhole bands

With RS facing and smaller needle, pick up and k 66 (70, 74) sts evenly around each armhole edge and work in St st for 4 rows. Bind off. Sew side seams including armhole band. Sew on buttons.

SKIRT

Measure fabric to desired length plus 1½"/4cm and cut across width of fabric. With RS tog, sew a ½"/1.25cm back seam. Press open. Press top edge under ¼"/1cm to WS twice. Sew in place. Rep for hem, pressing ½"/1.25cm under twice. Gather top edge of skirt to fit bodice. Hand-sew RS of skirt to WS of bodice.

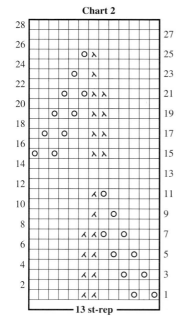

Chart 2

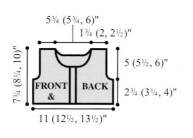

5¾ (5¾, 6)"
1¾ (2, 2½)"
5 (5½, 6)"
7¾ (8¼, 10)"
FRONT & BACK
2¾ (3¼, 4)"
11 (12½, 13½)"

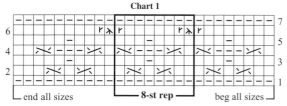

Chart 1

end all sizes — 8-st rep — beg all sizes

Stitch Key

☐ k on RS, p on WS   ⋏ SK2P

⊟ p on RS, k on WS   ⋊ RT

ᵣ M1   ⋉ LT

Stitch Key

☐ k on RS, p on WS   ⋏ k2tog

⊟ p on RS, k on WS   ⋏ ssk

◯ yarn over   ⋏ SK2P

13 st-rep

LADYBUG, LADYBUG

(Continued from page 86)

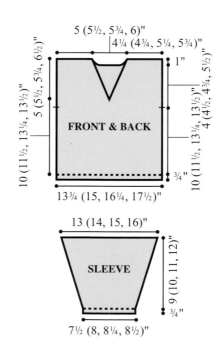

5 (5½, 5¾, 6)"
4¼ (4¾, 5¼, 5¾)"
1"
5 (5½, 5¾, 6½)"
10 (11½, 13¼, 13½)"
FRONT & BACK
4 (4½, 4¾, 5½)"
10 (11½, 13¼, 13½)"
¾"
13¾ (15, 16¼, 17½)"

13 (14, 15, 16)"
SLEEVE
9 (10, 11, 12)"
¾"
7½ (8, 8¼, 8½)"

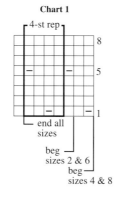

Chart 1

4-st rep

end all sizes
beg sizes 2 & 6
beg sizes 4 & 8

Stitch Key

☐ k on RS, p on WS

⊟ p on RS, k on WS

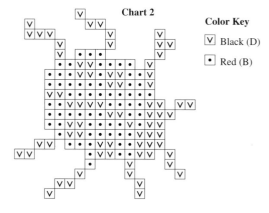

Chart 2

Color Key

ⱽ Black (D)

• Red (B)

Awesome Accessories

PANDA PALS

(Continued from page 92)

foll photo. Knit 40"/101.5cm length of I-cord. Sew each end of cord to side of purse. With A, make three 1½"/4cm pompoms. Sew 1 to each end of I-cord and to tip of flap.

TEEN SEEN

(Continued from page 96)

k1—10 sts. Cut yarn leaving long end for sewing. Pull through and draw up tightly and secure. Sew back seam.

FINISHING

Block lightly. With crochet hook, work an edge of sc around lower part of hat.

Twisted cord (make 3)

Cut 2 strands of yarn 28"/71cm long for each twisted cord. Attach cord to top and point of each earflap.

Tassels (make 3)

Wind yarn 30 times around cardboard that is 4½"/11.5cm wide. Secure at one end and cut other end. Wind 1 strand several times around tassel at 1"/2.5cm from top. Attach tassels to cords. (See page 90)

BAG

BACK

Cast on 38 sts. **Row 1 (RS)** K11, work next 16 sts in cable panel, k11. Cont in pat as established until piece measures 12"/30.5cm from beg. Bind off.

FRONT

Work as for back for 11½"/28.5cm. Bind off.

FLAP

Cast on 38 sts. Work as for back for 7½"/18.5cm. Bind off.

STRAP AND GUSSET

Cast on 8 sts. **Row 1 (WS)** *K1, wyif sl 1 purlwise; rep from *, end k2. Row 2 *P1, wyib sl 1 purlwise; rep from *, end p2. Rep these 2 rows for pat until piece measures 68"/173cm. Bind off.

FINISHING

Block pieces to measurements. Sew flap to top of back edge. Sew 2 short ends of strap tog. With strap seam at center of bottom of bag, sew strap around outer edge of bag for gusset to join front and back. With crochet hook, work

an edge of sc around flap with ch-10 lp for buttonloop at center. Work sc edge around front top edge. Sew on button.

WRAP STARS

(Continued from page 98)

and attach tassel. (See page 90)

GOLD SCARF

FINISHED MEASUREMENTS

■ Approx 12" x 48"/30.5cm x 122cm

GAUGE

11 sts to 4"/10cm over seed st.
TAKE TIME TO CHECK YOUR GAUGE.

SCARF

Loosely cast on 33 sts. Work in seed st for 48"/122cm Bind off loosely.

DARK BLUE SCARF

FINISHED MEASUREMENTS

■ Approx 6" x 48"/15.5cm x 122cm

GAUGE

11 sts to 4"/10cm over seed st.
TAKE TIME TO CHECK YOUR GAUGE.

SCARF

Loosely cast on 17 sts. Work in seed st for 48"/122cm Bind off loosely.

FEET FIRST

(Continued from page 100)

foll: **Row 1 (WS)** Sl 1 purlwise, p to end. **Row 2** *Wyib, sl 1 purlwise, k1; rep from * to end. Rep these 2 rows until heel piece measures 1"/2.5cm, end with a RS row. Turn heel.
Next row (WS) Change to B and sl 1, p8, p2tog, p1, turn. **Row 2** Sl 1, k3, SKP, k1, turn. **Row 3** Sl 1, p4, p2tog, p1, turn. **Row 4** Sl 1, k5, SKP, k1, turn. Cont in this way always having 1 more st before dec and SKP on RS rows, p2tog on WS rows until all sts have been worked—10 sts rem.

Shape instep

With same needle and cont with B, pick up and k 11 sts along side of heel piece (*Needle 1*); with *Needle 2*, k next 18 sts (instep); with *Needle 3*, pick up and k 11 sts along other side of heel piece, k 5 sts from first needle—50 sts. Mark center of heel for end of rnd. Resume working stripe pat as before. **Rnd 1** *Needle 1*, k to last 3 sts, k2tog, p1; *Needle 2*, knit; *Needle 3*, k1, SKP, k to end. **Rnd 2** Knit. Rep last 2 rnds 6 times

more—36 sts. Cont stripe pat, work even until foot measures 4 (5, 6)"/10 (12.5, 15.25)cm or 1½"/4cm less than desired length from back of heel to end of toe.

Shape toe

Working with B only, work as foll: **Rnd 1** *Needle 1*, K to last 3 sts, k2tog, kl; *Needle 2*. K1, SKP, k to last 3 sts, k2tog, k1; *Needle 3*. K1, SKP, k to end. **Rnd 2** Knit. Rep last 2 rnds 3 times more—20 sts. Place 10 sts on 2 needles and weave tog using Kitchener st.

FINISHING

Block socks, omitting ribbing.

COVER GIRL

(Continued from page 106)

Beg hand shaping

Next row (RS) K25, inc in next st, k1, inc in next st, k17—47 sts. Work 3 rows even. **Next row** K25, inc in next st, k3, inc in next st, k17—49 sts. Work 3 rows even.

Next row K25, inc in next st, k5, inc in next st, k17—51 sts. Work 3 rows even.

Next row K25, inc in next st, k7, inc in next st, k17—53 sts. P 1 row.

Thumb shaping

Next row K38, turn. **Next row** P12, turn, cast on 3 sts—15 sts.*** Work 16 rows on these 15 sts.

Top shaping

Row 1 *K1, k2tog; rep from * to end—10 sts.

Row 2 Purl.

Row 3 K2tog across—5 sts. Break yarn, run through rem sts and fasten off. With RS facing, pick up and k 3 sts from cast on sts at base of thumb, k to end—44 sts. Work 11 rows even, dec 2 sts evenly across last row—42 sts.

Index finger

Next row K27, turn.

Next row P12, turn, cast on 2 sts.***

Work 20 rows on these 14 sts.

Top shaping

Row 1 K2tog across—7 sts.

Row 2 Purl.

Row 3 K1, *k2tog; rep from * to end—4 sts. Break yarn, run through rem sts and fasten off.

Middle finger

With RS facing, join yarn and pick up and k 2 sts from cast-on sts at base of index finger, k5, turn.

Next row P12, turn, cast on 2 sts.

Work 24 rows on these 14 sts.

Top shaping

Work as for index finger.

Ring finger

With RS facing, join yarn and pick up and k 2 sts from cast-on sts at base of middle finger, k5, turn.

Next row P12, turn, cast on 2 sts.

Complete as for index finger from *** to end.

Little finger

With RS facing, join yarn and pick up and k 2 sts from cast-on sts at base of ring finger, k5, turn.

Next row P12.

Work 12 rows on these 12 sts.

Top shaping

Next row *K2tog; rep from * to end—6 sts.

Next row *P2tog; rep from * to end—3 sts.

Break off yarn, run through rem sts, draw up and fasten off securely.

Left Glove

Work to correspond to Right Glove, reversing placement of thumb and fingers. Beg hand shaping as foll:

Next row K17, inc in next st, K1, inc in next st, k25—47 sts.

FINISHING

Sew thumb, fingers and side seams.

ANTARCTIC TREASURES

(Continued from page 104)

2 sts tog—tuck made] twice, pass first st over st just worked; rep from * to last st, k1 —2 sts. ***

Row 6 P2, turn; cast on 5 sts—7 sts.

Rep from *** to *** once.

Next row P2, turn; cast on 4 sts—6 sts. Rep from *** to ***once. Pass first st over last; working along top edge of 'claws', pick up and p 6 sts (1 in top of each 'claw' and 1 in-between each)—7 sts. Beg with a k row, work 5 rows in St st.

Next row P1, p2tog tbl, p1, p2tog, p1. Bind off. With MC, cast on 5 sts, turn; with RS of 'claws' facing, pick up and k 6 sts from base of picked-up sts of foot, turn; cast on 5 sts—16 sts.

Next row P5, p2tog, p2, p2tog tbl, p5—14 sts. Work 4 rows in St st. Bind off. Sew back seam of leg, then tack foot to base of leg. Stuff firmly, then sew to front body at leg holes, adding additional stuffing to body if necessary.

UPPER RIGHT FLIPPER

With MC, cast on 24 sts.

Row 1 K, inc in last st.

Row 2 Inc in first st, p to end. Rep last 2 rows 3 times—32 sts. Mark beg of last row for top edge.

Row 9 K2tog, k to end.

Row 10 and all WS rows P to last 2 sts, p2tog.

Row 11 Bind off 2 sts, k to end.

Row 13 Bind off 3 sts, k to end.

Row 15 Bind off 4 sts, k to end.

Row 17 Bind off 11 sts, k to end—7 sts.

Rows 19 and 21 Rep row 9.

Row 23 K2tog twice. Fasten off.

UPPER LEFT FLIPPER

Work as for upper right flipper, reversing shaping.

UNDER FLIPPERS

With C1, work as for upper right and left flippers.

FINISHING

Sew pairs of flippers tog. Block flippers to flatten. Foll. photo, sew flippers to body, with front of top edge at markers. Mark position, then sew on eyes, stitching back and forth through head to secure.

BALLET CLASS

(Continued from page 108)

same length as back to underarm, shape left raglan armhole as for back.

RIGHT SLEEVE

With smaller needles, cast on 39 (41, 43, 45) sts. Work in k1, p1 rib pat for 2 (2, 2½, 2½)"/5 (5, 6.5, 6.5)cm, end with a WS row. Change to larger needles. Work in St st, inc 1 st each side every 6th row 4 (8, 6, 8) times, every 8th row 2 (0, 3, 3) times—51 (57, 61, 67) sts. Work even until piece measures 8½ (9¾, 12, 13½)"/21.5 (25, 30.5, 34)cm from beg, end with a WS row.

Cap shaping

Work as for back raglan armhole shaping until 31 sts rem, end with a WS row. Cont to dec 1 st at each side edge [alternately every 4th and 2nd row] twice more, AT SAME TIME, work as foll: **Next row (RS)** K11, k2tog, place marker (pm), ssk, k to end. Cont to dec 1 st each side of marker every other row 4 times more. When all decs have been worked and 13 sts rem, end with a WS row. **Next row (RS)** Bind off 4 sts, k to end. **Next row** P9. **Next row** Bind off 3 sts, k to last 3 sts, ssk, k1. **Next row** P5. **Next row** Bind off 2 sts, ssk. P2. Bind off rem 2 sts.

LEFT SLEEVE

Work as for right sleeve, reversing shaping at top of cap as foll: **Next row (RS)** K16, k2tog, pm, ssk, k to end. Cont to dec 1 st each side of marker every other row 4 times more. When all decs have been worked and 13 sts rem, end with a RS row. **Next row (WS)** Bind off 4 sts, p to end. **Next row** K9. **Next row** Bind off 3 sts, p to end. **Next row** K1, k2tog, k to end. **Next row** Bind off 2 sts, p to end. **Next row** K1, k2tog. Bind off rem 2 sts.

FINISHING

Block pieces lightly. Sew raglan sleeves to front and back raglan armholes. Sew sleeve seams. Sew side seams, leaving a ¾"/2cm opening in ribbing along right side seam, attaching seam at lower edge.

Sash loop

With crochet hook, leaving a 12"/30.5cm tail, ch 7 sts. Fasten off, leaving another 12"/30.5cm tail. Sew loop to left side seam at bottom and top of ribbing, securing ends.

(Continued next page)

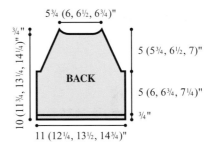

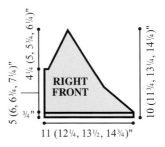

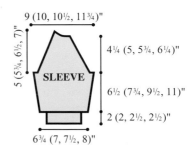

BALLET CLASS

(Continued from page 139)

Front band

With RS facing and smaller needles, pick up and k201 (225, 255, 273) sts evenly along front edges and along back neck edge. Work in k1, p1 rib for 4 rows. Bind off in rib.

Ties

Cut an 18"/46cm length of ribbon. Fold end under ¼"/.5cm and sew ¾"/2cm to inside of right front at corner. Cut a 30 (31, 32, 34)"/76 (79, 81, 86.5)cm length of ribbon and sew in same way to left front at corner. Pass left tie through opening in right side seam and loop, tie in a bow.

LEG WARMERS

FINISHED MEASUREMENTS

■ Width at upper leg 11¼ (12¾, 14, 15)"/28.5 (32.5, 35.5, 38)cm

■ Length 18½ (20, 21¾, 22)"/47 (51, 55, 56)cm

GAUGE

23 sts and 31 rows to 4"/10cm over St st, using size 4 (3.5mm) needles.
TAKE TIME TO CHECK GAUGE.

LEG WARMER

With smaller needles, cast on 49 (55, 59, 61) sts. Work in k1, p1 rib for 2½ (2½, 3, 3)"/6.5 (6.5, 7.5, 7.5)cm, end with a WS row. Change to larger needles. Work in St st (k on RS, p on WS), AT SAME TIME, inc 1 st each side every 10th (10th, 8th, 8th) row 4 (5, 3, 12) times, every 12th (12th, 10th, 10th) row 4 (4, 8, 1) times—65 (73, 81, 87) sts. Work even until piece measures 16 (17½, 18¾, 19)"/40.5 (44.5, 47.5, 48)cm from beg, end with a WS row. Change to smaller needles. Work in k1, p1 rib for 2¼ (2¼, 2¾, 2¾)"/6 (6, 7, 7)cm, end with a WS row. Make casing: **Next row (RS)** *K1, sl 1 st purlwise with yarn in front (wyif); rep from *, end k1. **Next row** P1, k1, *sl 1 st purlwise wyif, k1; rep from *, end p1. Rep last 2 rows once more. Cut yarn to approximately 4 times the width of piece. Thread yarn through tapestry needle and work tubular bind-off (see illustrations below).

FINISHING

Block piece lightly. Sew back seam. Thread tapestry needle with elastic. Carefully run elastic through casing at top of leg warmer. Adjust to comfortable fit, tie off elastic and run ends into casing.

TUBULAR BIND-OFF

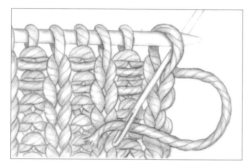

Step 1: Insert sewing needle knitwise into first knit st as shown. Drop st from LH needle. Pull yarn through the stitch.

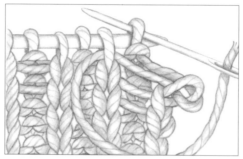

Step 2 and 3: Insert needle purlwise into third (K) st, then purlwise into second (P) st as shown. Drop second st from LH needle. Pull yarn through.

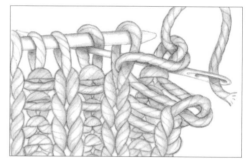

Step 4: Insert needle knitwise from the back of work into fourth (P) st as shown. Pull yarn through. Repeat steps 1-4.

THE TUTU GATHER

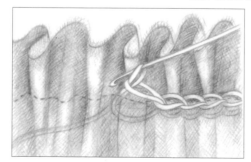

Step 1: First sew a line of basting to gather the tulle, then use a crochet needle to chain stitch along the basting.

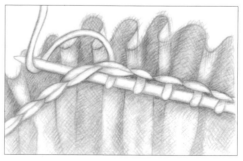

Step 2: Use a circular needle to pick up and knit through the loops formed by the chain stitches.

Crochet Cool

CAREFREE COMFORT
(Continued from page 114)

(inc by working 2 hdc in one st) every 5th row once, inc 6 hdc every 3rd row twice—92 hdc. When all stripes are completed, and collar measures approx 9½"/24cm, fasten off.

FINISHING
Block pieces to measurements. Sew shoulder seams. Place markers at 8½ (9, 9¼, 9½)"/21.5 (23, 23.5, 24)cm down from shoulders. Sew sleeves to armholes between markers. Sew side and sleeve seams. Beg at left shoulder seam, pin collar around neck edge along cast-on edge of collar. Sew collar around neck edge. Sew collar seam.

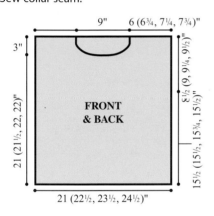

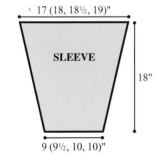

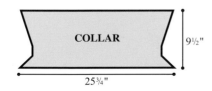

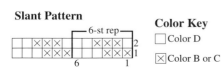

Slant Pattern

6-st rep

Color Key
☐ Color D
☒ Color B or C

TOO SWEET
(Continued from page 118)

NECK SHAPING
Next row (pat row 3) (RS) Skip first floral pat group and rejoin in top of 2nd cluster with a sl st to beg neck, ch 3, rep between °°'s twice into top of same cluster, yo and through all 3 lps on hook, then foll row 3 of pat between *'s only do not work first ch 3 at beg before dc, then work between *'s to end. **Pat row 4** Work pat row 4, end with 1 dc in 4th ch of last ch-7 arc, ch 3, rep between °°'s twice into same st as dc just worked, rep between °°'s 3 times into next ch-3 sp, yo and through all 6 lps on hook. **Pat row 5** Ch 3, rep between °°'s twice into center of first cluster pat group, yo and through all 3 lps on hook, work between *'s of row 5 to end. **Pat row 6** Work pat row 2 on 2 (3) floral pat groups, ending with yo and through all 6 lps on hook as in pat row 2. Work 0 (2) more rows. Fasten off.

LEFT FRONT
Rejoin yarn to work from WS of work and cont in pat st on last 4 (5) pats for 6 more rows, end with pat row 2, cut yarn.

NECK SHAPING
Work as for neck shaping on right front only, beg first row (pat row 3) on WS. Thus, the RS and WS are reversed (as pat is reversible) and the shaping is reversed. Complete as for right front.

SLEEVES
Beg at top edge of sleeve, with size G/6 (4.5mm) hook, ch 52 (60), work in pat st on 6 (7) floral pat groups until piece measures 6½"/16.5cm from beg and there are 10 rows in pat, end with pat row 2.

Dec shaping
Pat row 3 Ch 5, dc in top of next dc, ch 3, cont in pat, end with ch 3, dc in top of dc, double tr in top of cluster. **Row 4** Ch 3, 2 double tr in tr, 3 double tr in ch-3 sp, yo and through all 6 lps on hook, cont in pat, end with yo and through all 9 lps on hook. **Row 5** Ch 3, into center of cluster pat group work 2 double tr, yo and through 3 lps on hook, ch 3, dc in next dc then rep from * of pat row 5, end with ch 3, 3 double tr in top of the cluster, yo and through 4 lps on hook. **Row 6** Ch 3, 2 double tr in top of cluster, and 3 double tr in each ch-3 sp, yo and through all 9 lps on hook, cont in pat, end with double tr in edge st. **Row 7** Work row 3 of pat. Work even in pat on 4 (5) floral pat groups until piece measures 17"/43cm from beg. Fasten off.

FINISHING
Mist pieces with sprayer and allow to dry to measurements. Sew shoulder seams (or sl st tog from WS). Sew sleeves into armholes, closing up last ½"/1.3cm of armhole for large size only to accommodate top of sleeve. Sew sleeve seams.

EDGING
Working around sleeve cuff, work 2 rnds sc evenly around edge. Rnd 3 *Work 1 sc, 1 hdc, 1 dc, 1 hdc and 1 sc in first sc, ch 1, skip 2 sc; rep from * around. Join and fasten off. Work 3-rnd edge in same way all around lower, front and neck edges.

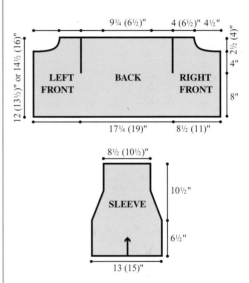

BATHING BEAUTIES
(Continued from page 112)

PONCHO
Work as for kerchief until there are 51 (53, 57) sts. Leave sts on holder. Cut yarn. Work a 2nd piece in same way, do not cut yarn. With circular needle, p51 (53, 57), then p51 (53, 57) from other piece—102 (106, 114) sts. **Next row** *K2tog tbl, yo; rep from * to end. Join and cont in rnds as foll: **Next rnd** Knit. Rep last 2 rnds for 6 (6½, 7)"/15.5 (16.5, 17.5)cm. **Next rnd** K2tog around—51 (53, 57) sts. [P 1 rnd, k 1 rnd] 5 times. Bind off loosely with larger needle.

FINISHING
Block piece lightly.

FRINGE
Cut 4 strands each approx 5"/12.5cm long for each fringe and attach to lower edge of poncho.

SQUARE DEAL

(Continued from page 120)

fold square 13 in half diagonally as indicated. Sew sleeves into armholes. For hood, sew squares 1-8 tog to form rectangle. Sew squares 9, 10, 11 to top of rectangle foll schematic, then join side of square 10 to top of square 2, top of square 10 to side of square 11 and top of square 9 to top of square 11 so that hood folds in half along fold line. To attach hood, join CC at top of right neck edge and work 80 dc evenly around entire neck edge. Fasten off. With CC, work an edge of dc evenly around entire face opening of hood. Sew neck edge of hood to neck edge of sweater. Beg at center of front slit, with CC work an edge of sc along neck edge, around entire face opening of hood and along other neck edge.

FLOWER TIE

With size G/6 (4.5mm) crochet hook and CC, ch 5, join with sl st to first ch to form ring. **Rnd 1** Ch 1, work 12 sc in ring, sl st to first sc. **Rnd 2** *Ch 3, [yo hook and pull up a lp in next sc, yo and through 2 lps] 3 times in same sc, yo and through all 4 lps on hook, ch 3, sl st in next 2 sc; rep from * 3 times more, end last rep by sl st in 1 sc, ch 130 for drawstring, then sl st in each ch and join with sl st to flower. Pull drawstring through dc row on neck. Make a 2nd flower, omitting drawstring, and sew to other end.

BAG

FINISHED MEASUREMENTS

◼ 15" long x 13½" wide/38cm x 34cm

GAUGE

1 square to 4½"/11.5cm using size H/8 (5mm) hook.
TAKE TIME TO CHECK YOUR GAUGE.

SQUARE I

Using colors A, B, C and D, make 9 squares foll instructions. Note that rnd 5 only uses A2 instead of A.

SQUARE II

Using colors A-2, B-2, C-2 and D-2, make 9 squares foll instructions. Note that rnd 5 only uses A instead of A-2.

GRANNY SQUARE

Beg at center, with size H/5mm hook and A (A-2), ch 4, join with sl st to first ch to form ring.

Rnd 1 With A (A-2), [work 1 sc in ring, ch 3] 4 times, join with sl st to first sc. Fasten off. **Rnd 2** With B (B-2), make a lp on hook, sl st into a ch-3 sp, ch 3 (counts as 1 dc), 2 dc, ch 3 and 3 dc in same sp for corner, *3 dc, ch 3 and 3 dc in next sp; rep from * twice, join with sl st to top of ch-3. Fasten off. **Rnd 3** With C (C-2), make a lp on hook, 1 sc in corner ch-3 sp, ch 3, 1 sc in same sp, *ch 3, 1 sc between 3rd and 4th dc's, ch 3, 1 sc, ch 3 and 1 sc in corner; rep from *, end last rep ch 3, join with sl st to first sc. **Rnd 4** With C (C-2), sl st into corner ch-3 sp, ch 3 (counts as 1 dc), 2 dc, ch 3 and 3 dc in corner, *3 dc in each ch-3 sp to next corner, 3 dc, ch 3 and 3 dc in corner; rep from *, end 3 dc in last sp, join with sl st to top of first ch-3. Fasten off. **Rnd 5** With A-2 (A), make a lp on hook, 1 sc in corner sp, ch 3, 1 sc in same sp, *ch 3, 1 sc between each of the next 3rd and 4th dc's; rep from * to next corner, ch 3, 1 sc, ch 3 and 1 sc in corner; rep from *, end ch 3, join with sl st to first sc. Fasten off. **Rnd 6** With D (D-2) make a lp on hook and rep rnd 4. Fasten off.

FINISHING

Working from WS of squares, using size G/6 (4.5mm) hook, sl st squares tog through back lps only, alternating squares I and II as in photo. Join 9 squares for front and 9 squares for back alternating pink and blue placement. Block finished pieces lightly.

TOP EDGE

With size G/6 (4.5mm) hook and A, working through back lps only, dec 9 sts evenly spaced to work 53 sc evenly along one edge. Turn. **Row 2** Ch 2, hdc in each sc, turn. **Row 3** Ch 1, sc in each st. Turn. **Row 4** With D-2, ch 5, *skip 2 sts, dc in next st, ch 3; rep from *, end dc in last st. **Row 5** With A, ch 1, and *working over ch-3 of previous row and into row 3 below, work 1 dc in each of next 2 sts, sl st in top of dc in D-2; rep from * to end. Do not fasten off, but cont as foll:

First side edge

Cont with A, work 5 sc into side of rows that form top edge, then work 53 sc through back lps (tbl) only (dec 9 as before) along side edge, then work 63 sc tbl evenly (no dec's) along lower edge, 53 sc tbl along other side edge (dec 9 sts), 5 sc along side of top edge, then ch 130 for strap. Join to top of other edge and cont in rnds as foll: **Rnd 2** Work 1 sc in each sc around edge, then 1 sc in each ch of strap. **Rnd 3** With D-2, working tbl only, sc in each sc. Fasten off.

SECOND SIDE EDGE

Working on other side edge of bag, work in same way as first side edge. Working through top lps only, sew strap and bag tog along center, using an overcast st from RS. Steam strap and side edges lightly.

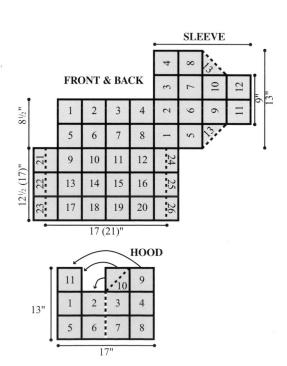

Resources

UNITED STATES RESOURCES

Baabajoes Wool Company
PO Box 26064
Lakewood, CO 80226
www.baabajoeswool.com

Berroco, Inc.
PO Box 367
Uxbridge, MA 01569

Brown Sheep Co.
100662 County Road 16
Mitchell, NE 69357
www.brownsheep.com

Caron International
200 Gurler Road Suite 1
DeKalb, IL 60115

Cascade Yarns, Inc.
2401 Utah Ave S Suite 505
Seattle, WA 98134

Classic Elite Yarns
300 Jackson Street Bldg. #5
Lowell, MA 01852

Cleckheaton
distributed by Plymouth Yarns

Colinette Yarns
distributed by Unique Kolours

Coats & Clark
Attn: Consumer Service
PO Box 12229
Greenville, SC 29612-0229
(800) 648-1479
coatsandclark.com

Filatura Di Crosa
distributed by Tahki•Stacy Charles, Inc.

JCA
35 Scales Lane
Townsend, MA 01469

Judi & Co.
18 Gallatin Drive
Dix Hills, NY 11746

King Cole
distributed by Cascade Yarns

Lane Borgosesia
PO Box 217
Colorado Springs, CO 80903

Lily ®
PO Box 40
Listowel, ON N4W 3H3
Canada

Lion Brand Yarn Co.
34 West 15th Street
New York, NY 10011
Customer Service: (800) 258-9276
lionbrand.com

Muench Yarns
285 Bel Marin Keys Blvd., Unit J
Novato, CA 94949-5724

Naturally
distributed by S.R. Kertzer, Ltd.

Patons®
PO Box 40
Listowel, ON N4W 3H3
Canada
patonsyarns.com

Plymouth Yarn
PO Box 28
Bristol, PA 19007

Reynolds
distributed by JCA

Rowan Yarns
5 Northern Blvd.
Amherst, NH 03031

S.R. Kertzer, Ltd.
105A Winges Road
Woodbridge, ON L4L 6C2
Canada
Tel: (800) 263-2354
www.kertzer.com

Steinbeck Wolle
distributed by Muench Yarns

Tahki Yarns
distributed by Tahki•Stacy Charles, Inc.

Tahki•Stacy Charles, Inc.
8000 Cooper Ave., Bldg. 1
Glendale, NY 11385
Tel: (800) 338-YARN
tahki@worldnet.att.net

Unique Kolours
1428 Oak Lane
Downingtown, PA 19335

Wool Pak Yarns NZ
distributed by Baabajoes Wool Co.

CANADIAN RESOURCES

Berroco, Inc.
distributed by S. R. Kertzer, Ltd.

Classic Elite Yarns
distributed by S. R. Kertzer, Ltd.

Diamond Yarn
9697 St. Laurent
Montreal, PQ H3L 2N1 and
155 Martin Ross, Unit #3
Toronto, ON M3J 2L9

Filatura Di Crosa
distributed by Diamond Yarn

Les Fils Muench
5640 Rue Valcourt
Brossard Quebec J4W 1C5

Lily ®
PO Box 40
Listowel, ON N4W 3H3
Canada

Patons®
PO Box 40
Listowel, ON N4W 3H3

Rowan
distributed by Diamond Yarn

S. R. Kertzer, Ltd.
105A Winges Rd.
Woodbridge, ON L4L 6C2

We have made every effort to ensure the accuracy of the contents of this publication.
We are not responsible for any human or typographical errors.

Acknowledgements

Many people contributed to the making of this book. In particular, and most importantly, we would like to thank all the past and present editors of *Family Circle Easy Knitting* magazine—including Nancy J. Thomas, Carla S. Scott, Margery Winter and Gay Bryant—for their vision and impeccable design selection. We would also like to extend our warmest gratitude to Barbara Winkler, Susan Kelliher Ungaro and Diane Lamphron from Family Circle for their inspiration and support. Lastly, we would like to extend our appreciation to all of the dedicated and knowledgeable knitters, designers, contributing technical experts and staff members who have worked on *Family Circle Easy Knitting*, without whom this book would not be possible.

Photo Credits

Paul Amato
17, 21, 27, 29, 35, 51, 55,
71, 73, 75, 77, 85, 93, 99,
103, 107, 113, 115, 119, 121,

Jim Jordan
37

Brian Kraus
11, 19, 33, 39, 43, 67, 109

Bruce Laurance
25, 91, 95, 97

VNU Syndications
9, 13, 15, 23, 57,

Nick Vaccaro
41, 45, 49, 104

Marco Zambelli
61, 63, 65, 69, 81, 87, 101, 117